A TREASURY OF
ILLUMINATED
MANUSCRIPTS

*A selection of miniatures from manuscripts
in the Austrian National Library*

FRANZ UNTERKIRCHER

G. P. PUTNAM'S SONS · NEW YORK

Frontispiece (Plate 1)

ANTIPHONARY OF ST PETER'S SALZBURG

SCOURGING OF CHRIST; DESCENT FROM THE CROSS

(see page 54)

FIRST AMERICAN EDITION 1967

TRANSLATED FROM THE GERMAN
ABENDLÄNDISCHE BUCHMALEREI
BY J. MAXWELL BROWNJOHN

PUBLISHED IN GREAT BRITAIN UNDER THE TITLE
EUROPEAN ILLUMINATED MANUSCRIPTS

LIBRARY OF CONGRESS CATALOG CARD NUMBER: 67-11394

THIS EDITION © THAMES AND HUDSON LONDON 1967
© STYRIA VERLAG GRAZ VIENNA COLOGNE 1966
COLOUR PLATES PRINTED BY
PHOTOCHEMIGRAPHISCHE UND XYLOGRAPHISCHE ANSTALT BEISSNER & CO, VIENNA
TEXT PRINTED IN THE NETHERLANDS BY MEIJER WORMERVEER

CONTENTS

VI ITALIAN ILLUMINATION
THIRTEENTH-SIXTEENTH CENTURIES   127

VII ILLUMINATION IN FRANCE AND ENGLAND
THIRTEENTH-FIFTEENTH CENTURIES   167

VIII ILLUMINATION IN THE NETHERLANDS FIFTEENTH-SIXTEENTH CENTURIES

IX LATE ILLUMINATION SIXTEENTH-CENTURY

FOREWORD

As heir and successor to the former Imperial and Royal Court Library, the Austrian National Library is one of the oldest in the world, and the all-embracing title of the present selection of miniatures, *European Illuminated Manuscripts*, is fully in keeping with the rich heritage which it has accumulated over the centuries. Roughly speaking, 'European' is taken to cover the territories which Charlemagne united under his personal dominion, that is to say, France, Germany, Bohemia, the former Kingdom of Lombardy, and the remainder of Italy.

Although this extensive area was often disrupted by political developments during the period that elapsed between Charlemagne's reign and the decline of book illumination in the sixteenth century, the basis of its civilization remained largely the same: Christian unity against a background of classical culture. This unity, which embraced the whole of the West, is vividly reflected in the following selection of miniatures. However much they may vary in style according to date and land of origin, and however much they differ in what they convey and how they convey it, they nonetheless belong to a single cultural domain – one which the latter-day European still distantly recognizes as home ground.

Of all the graphic arts, none is as obscure and unfamiliar as that of the illuminator. One reason for this is that it is no longer practised today: its place has been usurped by mechanical methods of reproduction which satisfy – indeed satiate – the world's ever-growing pictorial needs.

Another reason for the obscurity of book illumination is that examples of the art can seldom be exhibited to a wide public. Illuminated manuscripts are far frailer than panel-paintings or sculpture.

Some works of art are, by their very nature, destined for the public eye. They impinge on people as they walk the streets, demand their critical appreciation, mould their taste. Those who wish to see illuminated manuscripts by contrast, must go in search of them. Exhibitions are held from time to time and isolated specimens are on permanent show in large libraries, but the still, small voice of these little works of art often fails to penetrate the modern thunder of superlatives. They make special demands on those who wish to grasp their full richness, but they repay any effort expended on them. Their language is more personal than the language of larger pictures and their relationship with the beholder more intimate. A small picture confines its appeal to the person in front of it, whereas a large picture invariably addresses the world at large.

INTRODUCTION

The history of European book illumination begins with the emergence of the book in the West and ends with the gradual obsolescence of handwritten books in the sixteenth century. The beginnings of the art lie on the ill-defined frontier between antiquity and the Middle Ages, a period when gradual dissociation from Byzantium and from the continuing effects of Greek Byzantine cultural ties was succeeded by the slow growth, in Italy, of a cultural awareness at once Latin and West European. One of the few surviving relics of this early period is the fifth-century *Codex Argenteus* at Uppsala, a Gothic translation of the Bible by Bishop Ulfila inscribed in silver and gold on purple vellum and probably intended for Theodoric the Great.

Although very few pre-Carolingian miniatures of Italian or Merovingian French origin are still extant, a whole series of superb works originated in that part of the West which did not subsequently form part of the Carolingian empire, namely, England and Ireland. The pre-Carolingian miniatures now on German soil also derive from works of art introduced into the Continent by Anglo-Saxon missionaries.

The Austrian National Library's collection of Western illuminated manuscripts contains a few modest examples dating back to the sixth century. However, the really major works which are regarded as such a vital contribution to European book illumination date from the close of the eighth century onwards, when Carolingian illumination really came into its own.

The artistic embellishment of a book could be effected in several ways: ornamentally, calligraphically, and pictorially. In addition, a book's binding formed an integral part of its decorative treatment.

From the outset, the accepted subjects for embellishment were 'initials', that is to say, the large letters at the beginning of a book or individual sections of a book. Closely allied to the embellishment of initials was the script itself, often executed in coloured inks or, in the case of particularly sumptuous texts, gold.

Pictures are encountered either as independent illustrations – sometimes on a page of their own, sometimes incorporated in the text – or, very often, as part of initials.

The different elements which go to make up the decoration of a book permit of infinite variation. Some books have only one pictorial page, the text being written in straightforward script relieved by the occasional modest initial. In others, the text is introduced by a succession of gorgeous miniatures. Often, a pictorial page faces an equally decorative page adorned with a single initial. Pictorial illustrations may be scattered throughout a book, some of them as adjuncts to the text and others as ingenious marginal glosses which often have no direct bearing upon it. There are books with a predominantly pictorial content, books with a brief explanatory text or no text at all, books with no real pictorial embellishment whatsoever – 'merely' the fanciful shapes of initials whose ornamentation creates a strange artistic no-man's-land where geometrical shapes, scroll-work and strap-work become fused, transforming themselves into leaves and tendrils from which sprout the heads of animals and mythical creatures. Peopling this magic garden are dragons with birds' heads, lions and sirens, seemingly figments of a wanton imagination but often imbued with symbolic significance.

The artists had a wide range of colours at their disposal. Of these, vermilion was especially favoured for the drawn embellishment of initials. The term 'miniature' is derived from the Latin *minium*. Not until much later, when everyone had forgotten about the use of *minium*, or red oxide of lead, for purposes of book illumination, did the word 'miniature' come to be associated with the Latin word *minuere* (to reduce) and, thus, with pictures of very small dimensions. However, the term originally had nothing at all to do with the scale of a picture.

The paints employed in book illumination were principally of mineral origin, though some were vegetable pigments. Details of their manufacture and use were passed on down the centuries from one atelier to another and occasionally recorded in writing. One such manual was compiled in the eleventh century by a priest named Theophilus, much of it from earlier sources. His instructions are so precise that they can still be followed today.

The quality of the paints employed can be gauged from the state of preservation of most illuminated manuscripts. Discounting instances of severe damage, the luminosity of the pigments is still as strong as it was five hundred or a thousand years ago. This applies in particular to the gold leaf which was so widely and lavishly used, thin laminae being applied to a ground prepared with glue. Insulation from atmospheric effects has done a great deal towards preserving the colours, which is why not a single early or high medieval wall-painting has survived as successfully as contemporary examples of book illumination.

Who were the originators of these pictures and ornaments which still retain so much of their vivid colouring?

Very few names have been passed down to us, and we cannot always tell whether they belong to the scribe or painter. The arts of calligraphy and illumination were confined to monastery schools until well into the twelfth century. Lay scribes may possibly have been employed at the beginning of the great upsurge in book production, when manuscripts were copied at many places in Charlemagne's empire and on his instructions, but monasteries remained the sole repositories of this tradition in the centuries that followed. Not until the end of the twelfth century, when one or two European monarchs sponsored a sort of profane culture at their courts, did any demand arise for scribes and painters from the laity. From the thirteenth century onwards, books were commissioned by universities as well as kings and dukes.

Although the art continued to be practised in monasteries from the close of the thirteenth century until the decline of book illumination, most professional book illuminators were laymen who carried out their extensive commissions with the help of assistants. Hence, one can often distinguish, in one and the same work, between the hand of the master and that of a less experienced aide. Very few names have come down to us from the latter centuries of book illumination, and the finest masterpieces of French and Flemish illumination will always remain anonymous. Thus, instead of a work bearing its artist's name, an artist is known either by the name of his work or the patron who commissioned it.

In earlier centuries, books embellished with paintings belonged almost without exception to the liturgical and theological category. Charlemagne's empire, in which great works of European art were deliberately sponsored, was conceived of as a sort of earthly Kingdom of God whose Christian inhabitants were jointly governed by their secular monarch and the Pope. The finest works of art produced during the Carolingian period were churches and their appurtenances, foremost among which were sacred texts: the Bible – primarily the four Gospels and the Psalms – and the books required for divine office. People continued to concentrate on these works during the centuries that followed, when the art of calligraphy once more became the almost exclusive prerogative of monasteries. From the thirteenth century onwards, an ever-increasing number of profane books began to be adorned with paintings – medical and juristic works in the main, but also poetical works whose handwritten texts were illustrated with pictures. In the case of medical works, graphic illustration was in the interests of the subject matter. The miniatures in juristic works had no such objective justification, and may have been intended to alleviate the dryness of the content slightly, but in poetical works the content itself cried out for the addition of pictures to text.

The popularity of pictorial illustration soon developed to such an extent that sacred texts, too, came to be adorned with scenes which we should regard as wholly profane. Early medieval initials often embodied figures which had no bearing on the text, it is true, but they usually possessed some measure of symbolic significance. In the course of the centuries, they lost this deeper meaning and became welcome playthings of the imagination. The magnificent French and Dutch prayer-books of the fifteenth and sixteenth centuries are so lavishly adorned with illustrations of a sacred and profane nature that their real textual content is almost overwhelmed. Their excellent state of preservation is probably attributable in no small degree to the fact that they were treated from the outset as works of art rather than devotional works, and, as such, carefully preserved from wear and tear. Their owners regarded them as objects of value, much as they did precious stones and gold and silver plate.

The owners of early ecclesiastical books also prized them, but not as the kings of France and dukes of Burgundy were to do later on. Because of their content, which was the sole reason for their rich ornamentation, the gospel-books and antiphonaries in cathedrals and monasteries were regarded as sacred objects on a par with saintly relics. They were used for divine office only on major feast-days, when, in company with relics, they were exposed to the reverent gaze of the populace. This reverential treatment was largely responsible for their continuing survival. In many cases, small squares of silk were stitched to pages bearing large miniatures to protect them from any damage which might have resulted from the pressure of the page opposite.

People persisted in hand-painting books for quite a while after the art of printing had been discovered, so there are a large number of illuminated incunabula in existence. Painting was only gradually supplanted by woodcuts and copperplate engravings.

By the end of the fifteenth century and first few decades of the sixteenth, printing had practically ousted the handwritten book, yet some of the finest handwritten and hand-painted books in our possession date from this very period. There were numerous bibliophiles for whom the mechanical technique of letterpress printing was not enough. They still wanted books which belonged to them alone, not books of which identical copies were owned by thousands of other people. The book-illuminator's art stood so high in their estimation that not even the finest woodcut or copperplate engraving could hold a candle to it.

These late examples of illumination are still preserved on vellum, the medieval writing-material. Vellum is animal hide specially treated so that both sides, interior and exterior, become smooth and white enough to take text and pictures. The animals whose hide was used for this purpose were calves, sheep, goats, and – in very rare cases – donkeys. The word parchment derives from the town of Pergamum in Asia Minor, where the manufacture of parchment originated in the third century BC. The durability of the material is another reason why works inscribed and painted on it have readily survived intact for upwards of a thousand years. All but a handful of the miniatures reproduced in this volume were painted on vellum. Paper, which originated in the Far East, reached the Arabs first and was transmitted by them to Spain and Sicily in the twelfth and thirteenth centuries. It was first used and manufactured elsewhere in Europe during the fourteenth century and, on an increasing scale, during the fifteenth. The quality of these early papers is so good that illustrated books made of them have also survived extremely well, but parchment continued to be regarded as the finer material.

No one has yet written a general and comprehensive history of book illumination, though there are many individual works devoted to famous illuminated manuscripts, to illumination in particular countries, and to specific masters and schools. Unlike, say, the history of medieval mural- or panel-painting, examples of which are relatively limited, the history of book illumination embraces tens of thousands of paintings which could never be reproduced in their entirety, even in our own era of advanced printing techniques. Thus, an illustrated history of this kind must necessarily be selective.

What follows is a selection culled from a library which has accumulated many items representative of the principal schools of European book illumination.

The date of the Imperial Court Library's foundation is unknown. The first librarian whose deed of appointment still survives is the Dutchman Hugo Blotius, who assumed the post in 1575. He found himself in charge of a very extensive library which already contained thousands of handwritten and printed books.

Among them were manuscripts which had been in the possession of Austria's rulers since the fourteenth century, many of them executed at their behest. The major examples of Austrian book illumination were owned by the archdukes and emperors from the very first. Emperor Frederick III (d.1493), though generally uninterested in spiritual matters, was already the possessor of a notable collection of illuminated books which he prized for their artistic embellishment quite as highly as any product of the goldsmith's or jeweller's art. He also inherited masterpieces of Bohemian illumination dating from the time of King Wenzel (d.1419).

Frederick III's son, Emperor Maximilian I (d.1519), was a noted amateur of fine books. This love had been instilled into him at an early age by the fact that his school-books were magnificent examples of the illuminator's art. As a young prince, during his brief first marriage (1477–82) to Mary, daughter and heiress of the Duke of Burgundy, he had come to know and love the work of the Dutch illuminators. Some of their finest works came into his possession when he inherited Burgundy, but testamentary provisions stipulated that these books must remain in Flanders. Thus, although the Imperial Library already owned a number of them in Maximilian's day, they were not incorporated in it until much later, mainly by Austrian regents of the Netherlands.

Despite his love of books, Maximilian was an exceedingly bad librarian. A library accumulates books in one place, whereas Maximilian scattered them around. He had no permanent residence and spent all his time on the move, so the numerous books in his baggage were exposed to all the hazards of travel. In many instances, too, the emperor would present a close friend with some handsome volume which he happened to have with him. That is why books formerly owned by Maximilian are still occasionally offered for sale by dealers or private owners. The National Library did not reacquire one such book until 1931, when it was purchased from a London antiquarian.

A substantial number of books from the emperor's estate had accumulated at Innsbruck. They were removed from there during the sixteenth century by Archduke Ferdinand of the Tyrol (d.1596) and installed in his celebrated *Kunstkammer* at Schloss Ambras, not far away. When the Tyrolean branch of the Habsburg family became extinct in 1665, Emperor Leopold I inherited the Ambras estate. The current librarian, Peter Lambeck (1663–80), removed 583 manuscripts, together with a quantity of printed books, to Vienna. Apart from manuscripts formerly owned by Maximilian, Ferdinand of the Tyrol had acquired a large number of rare handwritten books from Germany and Bohemia.

Throughout the sixteenth century, Viennese scholars and diplomats had also been collecting books for the Imperial Library, some of them from monastery libraries in Austria and Germany and others from abroad. Prominent among these scholars and humanists were Cuspinian (d.1529) and Lazius (d.1565), also the historiographer Johannes Sambucus (d.1587), who purchased a number of valuable manuscripts, mainly in Italy. Numerous Greek manuscripts were acquired in Constantinople by the diplomat Augerius Busbecke.

The librarians of the seventeenth and eighteenth centuries were often encouraged in their activities by their emperors, who took a keen personal interest in the library. Leopold I (1658–1705) not only facilitated the acquisition of new items but was himself an enthusiastic library user. Lambeck reports that, despite his exacting official commitments, the emperor often found time to read rare books, and that he withdrew and returned them in the regulation manner. For example, before setting off for the Reichstag at Regensburg on 12 November 1663 he spent several hours in the library but carefully returned any borrowed books prior to his departure.

With the seventeenth century came the acquisition of the Ambras library, preceded in 1655 by the purchase of the Fugger library at Augsburg, which contained many precious manuscripts. The latter collection was conveyed to Vienna by water, packed in fifty-two casks and twelve chests.

Emperor Charles VI (1711–40) was responsible not only for building the new Court Library but also for making some of its most valuable and extensive acquisitions. 1720 saw the purchase of a library belonging to Prince Eugene's Adjutant-General, Baron Georg Wilhelm Hohendorff, and in 1737 Prince Eugene's own famous library was acquired from his heir a year after his death. A large proportion of the Court Library's most precious illuminated manuscripts originally came from these two collections.

Other rare manuscripts were presented to the emperors on various occasions and passed into the library's possession after their death. These include Leopold I's Golden Psalter, acquired from the chapter of Bremen cathedral.

In 1756 Vienna's University Library was amalgamated with the Court Library, to be followed in 1780 by the Vienna City Library. The Court Library benefited comparatively little from the monastic dissolutions which took place under Joseph II (1780–90), since most of the monastery libraries were incorporated in their respective provincial libraries. The only miniatures of value came from the monastery of Mondsee and the Adeliges Damenstift (Noblewomen's Convent) at Hall in the Tyrol, which had inherited various devotional books from the archduchesses who had resided there in the past. In 1806 the Principality of Salzburg was 'secularized' and the Salzburg cathedral library, containing a large number of Carolingian manuscripts, became merged with the Court Library.

The growth of the collection of manuscripts owned by the Court Library and its successor, the Austrian National Library, can be traced back for hundreds of years. The items accumulated during the past half-millennium or so stem from every branch of scholarship. The Library's thirty-five thousand manuscripts are important primarily for textual reasons. Only about ten per cent embody artistic embellishments, and many of these are straightforward initials. On the other hand, hundreds of the manuscripts are adorned, not merely with one miniature, but with dozens or even scores of them, and many contain page after page decorated with paintings of consummate artistry. So varied are the origins of the non-Austrian manuscripts that all European countries are represented, as well as the world of Byzantium and – in large measure, too – the Islamic East.

The following selection is confined to illuminated manuscripts of European origin. To select sixty miniatures from a total of more than ten thousand was no easy task, but the author has attempted to give representative examples of individual periods and national styles. In order to keep the selection as wide as possible, only one example has been chosen from each manuscript. The only exceptions to this rule are the 'Antiphonary of St Peter's', a twelfth-century masterpiece of European illumination, and the 'Prayer-book of Mary of Burgundy', the two reproductions from which occupy a special status in the history of Flemish illumination.

Pictures have been reproduced in their original dimensions wherever possible, though the large format of some originals has occasionally necessitated reduction or reproduction in part. Often, too, entire pages have been reproduced in which text is the dominant feature and ornamentation is confined to initials and decorative borders, but these are precisely the pages which reveal something of the special character of illumination, which was intended to supplement the written text and combine with it to form a meaningful unity.

Much has already been written about the manuscripts in the Austrian National Library, particularly its famous miniatures. It is not the aim of this publication to present a review of the specialized books and treatises which deal with the miniatures reproduced here, hence the omission of all bibliographical data. The following notes are designed to provide a brief introduction to the pictures and their original environment. The author of the notes wishes to express his thanks to all the writers whose works he has drawn on for this purpose but whom he cannot mention by name because the selective nature of this volume precludes him from doing so.

I
PRE-ROMANESQUE ILLUMINATION
EIGHTH–ELEVENTH CENTURIES

Plate 2

CUTBERCHT GOSPELS

205 leaves, 12⅛ × 9¼ ins
4 full-page miniatures, 8 pages of Canon tables, 5 large initials
Written in Salzburg at the end of the eighth century by the
Anglo-Saxon monk Cutbercht
Cod. 1224

MARK THE EVANGELIST
FOL. 71ᵛ. SLIGHTLY REDUCED

red, green and brown, and the vellum is left bare at only a few points. Instead of capitals, flat slabs form the transition from pillars to arch, the latter being divided into three fields. The two outer fields are filled with undulating leaf-work and the one in the centre is painted monochrome violet.

The frame shuns any attempt at plasticity and preserves a wholly two-dimensional approach, but the painter is a master of the varied scroll-work which was so popular in the Anglo-Saxon domain.

The treatment of the Evangelist is strongly influenced, not only by its model, which was probably Byzantine, but by the established conventions of Insular art. The interior drawing of the under- and over-garments recalls the tendency of Anglo-Saxon painters to reduce the human form to a system of bands and stripes. The manner in which St Mark holds the book in both hands encourages one to assume that the original on which the painting was modelled depicted the book resting on a lectern. The bare space beneath the fore-quarters of the lion with the book also suggests that something is missing, but none of these minor flaws detracts fundamentally from the magnificent general effect of this full-page miniature. The robust figure of the Evangelist and his grave expression as he gazes across the open book convey some idea of the personalities of the missionaries who sallied forth from the seclusion of their Anglo-Saxon monasteries to proclaim their faith – and possibly die for it – in an alien land.

In ornamentation, the Cutbercht Gospels are closely related to another famous gospel-book of Austrian provenance, the so-called *Codex Millenarius* of Kremsmünster. It was earlier assumed that the Kremsmünster gospel-book was a transcript of the Cutbercht Gospels, and that its pictures of the Evangelists were copied from it. However, close scrutiny of text and artistic ornamentation has disclosed that the two gospel-books were based on a common antecedent and are roughly contemporaneous. They were probably written at the end of the eighth century, the Cutbercht Gospels at Salzburg and the Kremsmünster Codex in the monastery there.

The Cutbercht Gospels remained in their place of origin, the cathedral library at Salzburg, until 1806, when the ecclesiastical principality of Salzburg was 'secularized' and passed into the possession of the Austrian Crown. The bulk of the cathedral library was then transferred to the Imperial Court Library.

Plate 3

'THE GOLDEN PSALTER' (DAGULF PSALTER)

161 leaves, $7\frac{1}{2} \times 4\frac{3}{4}$ ins
5 decorative pages in gold majuscules on a crimson
or dark-blue ground
or in silver majuscules on a steel-blue ground
numerous initials in several colours
Written between 783 and 795 at the Carolingian court school (Aachen?)
Cod. 1861

DOUBLE-PAGE SPREAD
BEGINNING OF THE 51ST PSALM
FOL. 67ᵛ–68ʳ. ORIGINAL SIZE

parison with the Godescalc Evangelistary, completed in 783, suggests that the Golden Psalter must have been produced subsequently, which would place its date of origin somewhere in the twelve years between 783 and 795.

We also know the name of the scribe, who identifies himself in an introductory poem addressed to Charlemagne:

'Rex pie, dux sapiens, uirtute insignis et armis...
Exigui famuli dagulfi sume laborem...'
(Pious king, wise leader, renowned in virtue and arms...
accept the work of thine humble servant Dagulf...)

We meet two other references to Dagulf in the literature of the late eighth century. On one occasion, a scribe and painter extols him as a teacher, and in the period 789–96 the celebrated Alcuin writes to the elderly 'scriniarius' Dagulf and speaks of the warm friendship which existed between them when they lived at the same place. Where was this 'same place'? Was it the place where the psalter and several other books of the same group were written? Scholars think it probable that this renowned school of calligraphy actually operated at Charlemagne's court, where the close proximity of that royal patron of the arts would have facilitated the production of manuscripts lavishly adorned with gold, silver and purple regardless of cost. Artists at court would also have been stimulated in manifold ways by foreign works of the finest execution, gifts to the king from Rome and Byzantium. Thus, although no documentary evidence has yet come to light, it is highly probable that the Golden Psalter originated at the Palace school in Aachen.

Here it was that the book received its sumptuous binding – one whose spirit and appearance accorded with its content. Dagulf in his introduction describes this cover, which bore ivory reliefs depicting David in the role of royal singer. Psalter and binding are no longer together. The latter is preserved at the Louvre in Paris, though its date of arrival there can no longer be established.

The psalter's route to Vienna is equally difficult to trace with certainty. It first appears in the inventories of the Imperial Court Library in 1669, and the assumption is that it was presented to Emperor Leopold I by the chapter of Bremen Cathedral a few years earlier. Inscriptions on pages bound into the front during the seventeenth century indicate that it was then in the cathedral treasury, but we can only guess at how it got there. According to one version, the Pope presented it to Charlemagne's wife, Hildegard, who then bequeathed it to Bremen Cathedral. According to another, the psalter went to Rome and remained there until well into the eleventh century, when one of the Popes presented it to young Henry IV, who is known to have possessed a 'golden psalter'. Henry is then said to have presented it to Bishop Adalbert of Bremen (1043–72).

Whatever the truth, the Golden (or Dagulf) Psalter remains one of the few books which not only passed through the hands of prominent historical figures but were destined, by virtue of their lettering and presentation, to set an example which endured for centuries.

Plate 4

CAROLINGIAN GOSPELS FRAGMENT

1 sheet, $11\frac{1}{9} \times 7\frac{7}{8}$ ins
Late eighth century, displaying Carolingian Palace school motifs
Cod. Ser. N. 3201

FIRST PAGE OF ST MARK'S GOSPEL
FOL. 1ʳ. ORIGINAL SIZE

interlace of coloured bands. Superimposed on the lower part of the curve is a blue ornament shaped like a bird's wing, and the free space inside the letter is occupied by the entirely unadorned 'M' which completes the word.

Distributed over the rest of the page are the words of the opening sentence, all inscribed on a yellow-tinted ground. The word 'EVANGELII' is given special prominence, but the ensuing words are written in the sort of neat uncial script that had been traditionally used for sacred texts since the fifth century. This script is confined to the first page of the Gospel, however. The continuation of the text on the reverse side is not inscribed in the Carolingian minuscules first cultivated at the Palace school and early exemplified by the Golden Psalter, but in the so-called Insular minuscules used at the German schools of calligraphy founded by Anglo-Saxon missionaries of the eighth century. Among these were Fulda, Würzburg, and Mainz. The sheet under examination has nothing in common with extant Fulda manuscripts, so it probably originated further west, perhaps at Mainz. 'Perhaps' is about as far as one can go in ascertaining its place of origin. Individual features of its ornamentation undoubtedly derive from the Carolingian court school and, more especially, from early works of the 'eighties and 'nineties, but the juxtaposition of those features, augmented by one or two special motifs, is unique to this particular sheet.

For example, manuscripts produced by the Palace school often have medallions containing heads or busts in the stems of their initials. Small medallions containing silhouetted figures are far from rare, either, but there is no other instance of a head and silhouettes in combination. Three-dimensional mazes and white-dotted blue grounds often occur, too, as do stems culminating in intricate patterns of coloured bands, but characters constructed wholly of variegated animals' bodies, such as the 'N' formed by the two fish and the dog, are nowhere else to be found.

The use of Palace school ornaments proves that the author of this sheet was familiar with such works. He did not quite succeed in imitating their delicacy, nor did he always comprehend their meaning, hence the near-demonic appearance of the silhouettes on either side of the Evangelist's head. The mysterious 'dog' belongs to a style of ornamentation alien to the art of the Carolingian court, so the artist should probably be sought in an environment where the Insular minuscule was in current use but examples of Carolingian court art were also known.

Though unique, this sheet is not the only one in the whole gospel-book to have survived. Three sheets are in Munich, six in Stuttgart, several smaller fragments in Würzburg and one sheet in a private collection in New York, but all these sheets and fragments are entirely unadorned and bear nothing but passages of text written in neat minuscules. Only the Vienna sheet has this unique decorative page.

The Austrian National Library made this valuable acquisition in autumn 1962.

Plate 5

ASTRONOMICAL AND CHRONOLOGICAL TEXTS

165 leaves, 12⅝ × 9¾ ins
34 miniatures and 6 astronomical drawings
Produced at Salzburg prior to 821
Cod. 387

CONSTELLATIONS FROM AN ASTRONOMICAL TREATISE
FOL. 120ʳ. SLIGHTLY REDUCED

Arn became Bishop of Salzburg in 785. A close friend of Charlemagne, he was promoted archbishop at the king's instigation in 798, became a member of the committee of inquiry which Charlemagne dispatched to Rome in 799 to investigate charges made against the Pope, and was present when Charlemagne was crowned emperor at Christmas in the year 800.

Much of the book is devoted to a study of the 'computus' or calendar tables whose main function was to determine the date of the Easter festival. Also within the scope of this chronological treatise comes a study of the constellations and of one of the definitive scientific works of the Middle Ages, 'De natura rerum' (On the nature of things), written by the Venerable Bede, the erudite English monk who died in 735. One section of the book deals with the fixing of Easter from the year AD 1 to 1063. Against various years up to and including 1049, contemporary hands have noted sundry events in the history of the world and of the diocese of Salzburg – an indication that the book remained in use for centuries and was employed as an aid to the dissemination of theological knowledge at Salzburg. One pointer to the book's date is its script, which is a fully developed Carolingian minuscule of the sort used at Salzburg throughout the first half of the ninth century. Since 809 is referred to as 'the present year' in the brief chronicle of the world, this particular section must have originated either during or after that year. Again, since Arn's ordination as Bishop was recorded, but not – as in the case of later bishops – the date or year of his demise, the book was probably completed during Arn's lifetime, or prior to 821.

The Bavarian State Library in Munich owns a second copy of the same book. This came from Salzburg to the Abbey of St Emmeram in Regensburg, and later passed into the possession of Hartmann Schedel, the Nuremberg physician. It is probable that both books were copied at Salzburg from a manuscript which Bishop Arn brought with him from St Amand, his former abbey in Northern France.

In company with many other books, the Vienna copy was acquired by the Imperial Court Library from the cathedral library of Salzburg when the city was secularized in 1806.

Plate 6

HRABANUS MAURUS, 'DE LAUDE CRUCIS'

47 leaves, 16 × 11¾ ins
2 full-page miniatures, 30 figurative panels (illustrated poems)
Fulda, between 831 and 840
Cod. 652

HRABANUS MAURUS PRESENTING HIS BOOK TO POPE GREGORY IV
FOL. 2ᵛ. ORIGINAL SIZE

'PONTIFICEM SUMMUM SALUATOR CRISTE TUERE
ET SALUUM NOBIS PASTOREM IN SAECULA SERUA
PRESUL UT EXIMIUS SIT RITE GREGORIUS ALMAE
ECLESIAE CUSTOS DOCTORQUE FIDELIS IN AULA'
(Protect, O Christ Saviour, the Supreme Pontiff
and preserve the shepherd for us for ever,
that Gregory fitly be an excellent superior
of the bountiful Church, its guardian,
and a faithful teacher in the hall of learning.)

The Pope in question, Gregory IV (827–44), is seated on a red cushion in the centre of a bench, his blue robe covered by an alb, a green overgarment and a pallium. He is taking the book proffered by Hrabanus in his right hand. Hrabanus himself wears an undergarment of the same colour as the Pope's, and over it a short yellow-brown habit complete with cowl. Behind the Pope stand two deacons wearing white dalmatics over their blue undergarments. Hrabanus and the deacons are heavily tonsured in a style which differs from that of the Pope. The figures and the papal throne are superimposed on a yellow ochre ground. The broad pale blue band behind it is presumably intended to represent a back wall, and the strip of darker blue suggests the sky.

The miniatures are executed in body-colours and boldly outlined in black or red. Modelling is conveyed by the application of flat white high-lights or by varying the shade of the natural colour employed. The interior drawing of the faces has been applied in heavy black lines. Heads and hands are noticeably over-size. As for the author, under whose supervision and direction the codex was written and embellished, his figure undoubtedly has the attributes of a portrait. Since Pope Gregory IV had paid a personal visit to the emperor in the year 833, it is possible that his features, too, were based on reality.

The style of the dedicatory pictures is far removed from the elegance of the Palatine style cultivated under Charlemagne. Although references dating from the turn of the century were available, the Fulda artists contributed a great deal that was their own. Under Abbot Hrabanus, Fulda became not only a centre of learning but also an important art centre. A great deal of building was done there, and the new buildings were adorned with paintings. Sumptuous reliquaries were produced and books illuminated there. One Fulda artist whose name we know was Hatto, a monk, underwent his training at Tours with Hrabanus and was probably the first man to illustrate the original edition of the present work, which was completed *c*. 806. We meet later references to a biography of the monk Eigil, a friend of Hrabanus; this was adorned with miniatures by a monk named Modestus. Modestus, who was a contemporary of Hrabanus, i.e. roughly fifty years old between 831 and 840, may also have been responsible for the dedicatory paintings, unless, of course, they were produced by Hatto himself.

This rare manuscript used to be in St Stephen's Abbey at Würzburg during the fifteenth century, but had arrived in the Imperial Court Library by 1576.

Plate 7

CAROLINGIAN SACRAMENTARY FRAGMENT

8 leaves, 10⅞ × 8½ ins
8 decorative frames, 2 pages of elaborate ornamental lettering
Northern France, *c.* 860
Cod. 958

ORNAMENTAL PAGE BEARING THE WORD 'TE'
FOL. 5ᵛ. ORIGINAL SIZE

One of them was produced for the Abbey of St Denis and is now in Paris, and another, now in Stockholm, was destined for the Abbey of St Amand. The nineteen manuscripts so far identified as belonging to this group were produced *c*. 860 in Northern France or Southern Belgium, possibly at the St Vaast scriptorium in Arras. They are among the finest illuminated manuscripts produced in Northern France during the reign of Charles the Bald (d. 877).

We do not know for whom this particular sacramentary was originally intended. Additions to the saints listed in the text of the Canon – St Lambert is twice mentioned in a late ninth-century entry – suggest that the book was in use in Liège during that period. Other addenda made in the tenth century refer to saints who were only venerated in Lombardy. One note – almost obliterated – states that the book was in the monastery at Bobbio (Northern Italy).

Since there are one or two tenth-century manuscripts from Bobbio whose ornamentation and ornamental lettering bear a close affinity to this sacramentary, we may assume that the book was already there by the tenth century.

So splendidly illuminated was the manuscript that it aroused the interest of bibliophiles as early as the sixteenth century. Among its owners were Cardinal Girolamo Seripando, Archbishop of Salerno (d. 1563), and, later, Antonio Folch de Cardona (d. 1724), Archbishop of Valencia, who bequeathed his library to the Franciscans of that city. It was from them that Emperor Charles VI purchased the slim manuscript for his Court Library. One of its seventeenth-century owners had it bound in costly gold brocade.

Plate 8

LIFE OF ST ULRICH

137 leaves, 8 × 6 ins
One full-page miniature and several initials
Produced at Reichenau or Augsburg, *c.* 1020–30
Cod. 573

St Ulrich of Augsburg flanked by Abbot Berno of Reichenau and
Abbot Fridebold of St Ulrich and Afra in Augsburg
Fol. 26ᵛ. Original size

II

ILLUMINATION IN AUSTRIA
TWELFTH CENTURY

Plate 9

ADMONT GIANT-BIBLE

2 volumes of 262 and 234 leaves respectively, 22 × 16⅛ ins
46 miniatures and 117 initials of various sizes
Salzburg, *c.* 1140
Cod. Ser. N. 2701–2702

JOB WITH HIS WIFE, TWO FRIENDS, AND A MAIDSERVANT
FROM VOLUME I OF THE ADMONT BIBLE
FOL. 252ᵛ. REDUCED

art. The foliate scroll-work of the initial, applied in pale brushed gold, reposes on a background which already displays the strange conjunction of blue and green so brilliantly utilized in the Antiphonary of St Peter's a decade or two later.

The illuminators of this Bible were members of the atelier which worked on the walls of the church of Nonnberg in Salzburg at about the middle of the twelfth century. Indeed, the mural painters and book illuminators may have been identical. The stylistic affinities between the Nonnberg frescoes and the miniatures under discussion also help to identify the Bible's place of origin as Salzburg and date it to the period shortly before the middle of the twelfth century.

Known as the *Riesenbibel*, or 'giant Bible', by reason of its dimensions, this manuscript remained for hundreds of years at the Abbey of Admont, where it may have arrived at the beginning of the fourteenth century or shortly thereafter. The first volume contains forty large-scale miniatures and forty-one large initials. Two sheets of miniatures were lost very early on and found their way at some stage into the Ecole des Beaux-Arts in Paris. The second volume contains six miniatures and seventy-six initials of various sizes. Several half-pages and smaller areas were left blank for the addition of miniatures. The lettering is a large but somewhat irregular Romanesque book script. Even though the embellishment of the Bible was never quite completed, it remains a monumental piece of illumination and one of the prime mid-twelfth-century examples of the illuminator's art.

Some doubt attaches to the initial stages of the Bible's career, but it probably went to the Monastery of St Peter at Csatár in Western Hungary at an early date – indeed, the founder of the monastery, a Count Martinus, may actually have ordered the work direct from Salzburg. Entries on blank pages in the first volume inform us that both volumes were pawned to a Jew named Farkasius, and the handwriting in question dates from the thirteenth century. We know from other documents that the Abbot of Zala, who also held the benefice of Csatár, made a number of bequests to the latter monastery in restitution for the loss of a Bible which he had pledged to the Jew Farkasius in an emergency and never redeemed.

Two leaves bound into the front of the first volume bear a rhymed catalogue of the Archbishops of Salzburg up to and including Eberhard III (1403–27) and a rhymed catalogue of the Abbots of Admont up to Hartnid (1391–1411), so the Bible must have been in Admont at the beginning of the fifteenth century. Quite when it arrived, no one can tell. Perhaps it was sold to the monastery by the Jew Farkasius. Since Abbot Engelbert of Admont (1297–1327) was an enthusiastic bibliophile, it could have been he who acquired the famous work.

The book was held in high esteem at Admont. Abbot Antonius had the two volumes re-bound in 1737 and adorned the covers with his coat of arms. Financial difficulties compelled the abbey to sell its treasured possession to the Austrian government in 1937.

Plate 10

LIUTOLD GOSPELS

192 leaves, 11⅜ × 7⅝ ins
12 miniatures of which 7 full-page, 4 large ornamental pages
15 fairly large and numerous smaller initials
Written and illuminated at Mondsee Monastery by the monk Liutold
Third quarter of the twelfth century

CHRIST IN LIMBO; CHRIST APPEARS TO MARY AND THOMAS
FOL. 189ʳ. ORIGINAL SIZE

'Liutoldus monachus, qui multa labore patrauit,
scripsit et istud opus, pro posse suo decorauit.
Signifero caeli delegans mente fideli.'
(The monk Liutold, who accomplished many things with toil,
wrote this work, too, and adorned it to the best of his ability,
dedicating it with a loyal mind to the Standard-bearer of Heaven
[St Michael, principal patron saint of Mondsee].)

The book contains a total of twelve miniatures, seven of them full-page, as well as four large illuminated pages bearing the initial letters of the four Gospels, fifteen sizable initials and numerous smaller initials in gold and colour. Stylistically and iconographically, Liutold was heir to the Salzburg illuminators of the late eleventh century, so these Mondsee paintings of the mid-twelfth century create an impression of greater age than Salzburg miniatures of the same period or even earlier (cf. the Admont Giant-Bible and the Antiphonary of St Peter's). It is probable that Liutold only had earlier references at his disposal.

The picture reproduced here comes from the Gospel according to St John. The scenes are enclosed by a frame displaying features which recall large Italian Bibles of the period. Sandwiched between a blue outer border and a reddish-orange inner border is a spiral pattern outlined in black and divided into sections of pale green, ochre, and crimson.

The scenes are disposed on two levels within this frame. The larger, upper portion is devoted entirely to Christ's descent into Limbo. Christ, identified by a cruciform nimbus and escorted by two angels, strides towards the open gate of Hell from left to right. His left hand grasps the banner of the Re-surrection and his right hand the raised right arm of Adam, who is shown with Eve emerging from the fiery glow. On the right is a portrayal of the interior of Hell, a brown mountain with tongues of flame spurting from fissures in its sides. Within, surrounded by serpents, is Satan, pictured as a monster with a grotesque head and the talons of a predator, his hands and feet bound fast in a red mesh whose strange convolutions recall the patterns on illuminated initials. The lower, smaller section embodies two scenes side by side: on the left, Christ manifesting himself to Mary Magdalene; on the right, Thomas laying his hand on the wound in Christ's side.

The background of the pictures is executed in gold – not gold-leaf but gold paint applied with a brush like any ordinary pigment. The range of colours employed is unusually wide: several shades of vermilion and wine-red, a yellowish orange-red, rose-red, crimson, pale sky-blue, turquoise, pale ultramarine, pale green, olive-green, grass-green, yellow, violet and brown – all invest the miniatures with considerable variety. One characteristic feature of Liutold's facial modelling is that he stresses the lips with small specks of red and the cheeks with somewhat larger ones. Where drapery is concerned, he is fond of depicting figures clad in several superimposed garments which differ in colour and texture and of which the lining often differs in colour from the facing. Characteristic, too, are the small T-shaped folds in the hems of the robes and in the shawl draped over Mary's right shoulder.

Our limited knowledge of Liutold's work suggests that this gospel-book should be dated in the period c. 1160. Another gospel-book, lettered and illuminated by Liutold for the monastery of Ranshofen and now in Oxford, is dated c. 1178.

The Mondsee evangeliarium was acquired by the Imperial Court Library when the monastery was dissolved in the reign of Joseph II.

Plates 1 (Frontispiece) and 11

ANTIPHONARY OF ST PETER'S, SALZBURG

846 leaves, 17 × 12⅛ ins
14 full-page and 2 half-page miniatures and initials in gold and colour
12 richly embellished Calendar pages, 50 half-page pen-drawings
in dark violet and sepia ink against a green and blue background
more than 400 initials in sepia and blue ink on a green and blue background
numerous unadorned initials in red and blue
Salzburg, c. 1160
Cod. Ser. N. 2700
ADORATION OF THE KINGS; BAPTISM OF CHRIST
PAGE 198. REDUCED
ORIGINAL SIZE 11⅝ × 8¼ ins
(Frontispiece)

SCOURGING OF CHRIST; DESCENT FROM THE CROSS
PAGE 630. REDUCED
ORIGINAL SIZE 12 × 8½ ins

such magnificent works, knowing full well that few people would ever set eyes on them? This particular antiphonary was not there for anyone to dip into, but was used exclusively at divine service on feast-days. Choristers had little time or opportunity to dwell on the miniatures or study the complex tracery of the initials. The congregation could only catch a distant glimpse of the book as it lay open in the choir. The abbot may occasionally have permitted a celebrated visitor to inspect the book, but it was not for man that the artists gave of their best. The abbot dedicated the book to St Peter. The Word of God embodied in it and the songs of praise that were sung from it deserved the finest embellishment of which man was capable. Whether or not man took pleasure in it was of secondary importance. The purpose of this sacred form of art, for which human gratification and approbation held little or no significance, was to glorify God.

The first picture selected from the antiphonary is taken from the decorative pages for major feast-days. At Epiphany, the manifestation of Our Lord, the Church celebrates three incidents from Christ's life: the Adoration of the Kings; the Baptism in the Jordan, at which a voice from heaven proclaimed Jesus to be the Son of God; and the Wedding in Cana, where Jesus performed the miracle which revealed his divine power for the first time. The antiphonary depicts the latter scene in a pen-drawing, whereas the first two are portrayed in the two pictorial strips accompanying the Mass for Epiphany.

Enclosed by a frame of variegated palmettes, the pictorial field is divided into two halves by a blue band. Gold invests the background with due solemnity. Visible in the top left corner are the walls and slender tower of a city gate-house, and before it stands the throne of the Mother of God surmounted by an arched baldachin supported on pillars of the sort found in earlier Byzantine miniatures. The poses adopted by the Virgin and Child also recall Byzantine antecedents. There is nothing particularly childish about the face of Christ, who extends a benedictory hand towards the Wise Men with an air of majesty. The Virgin is holding the Child with one hand while stretching out the other to accept the proffered gifts.

The Virgin's throne reposes on a low plinth adorned with foliate scroll-work. The ground to the right of it undulates slightly and is dotted with a few clumps of grass. The Three Wise Men are arranged one behind another in various animated poses. The first is captured in the act of genuflecting. To prevent his red gold from spilling during this obeisance, he holds one hand over it protectively. The exalted status of the old man, who wears a mitre-like head-dress adorned with a narrow red border, is proclaimed by his gorgeous apparel. Behind him stands a young man identified as a king by a mural crown of the sort customarily worn by personifications of cities in ancient times. The position of his feet, which are clad in pale green hose, indicates that he is just taking his final step towards the throne. Behind the third king flutters the hem of his reddish cloak, caught by the wind. He is also depicted walking at a rapid pace, hence the way the gorgeous material billows out behind. His face is bearded, and he is wearing a red cap trimmed with gold. He holds the bowl containing his gift in his left hand, supporting it with the right.

The lower picture is entirely dominated by the figures of Christ and, standing humbly before him, John the Baptist. Christ stands chest-deep in the waters of the Jordan, whose denizens regard him with awe. His head is bowed and his right hand raised in a gesture of benediction. John, dressed in a cloak of variegated skins, is touching his forehead respectfully with his right hand and has extended his left as though timidly contemplating physical contact. He seems to be staring past the Messiah's head at the Dove with its flame-red aureole, while simultaneously listening to the words of God the Father. Leaning towards Christ from the right-hand edge of the picture is an angel, who offers him a towel adorned with red crosses and circular designs in blue, and approaching from the left-hand side are several awestruck onlookers.

The aureoles round the figures in both the upper and lower pictures are scratched into the gold background in the style of a Byzantine miniature.

The Epiphany picture is incorporated in the first part of the antiphonary, which contains the variable liturgical songs appointed to be sung at Mass. Also reproduced here is a page of pictures for Holy Week taken from the pen-drawings in the second part, with its sacred songs. Between the antiphons for lauds (the morning office) on Saturday in Holy Week and for vespers of the same day, which provide a transition to the rejoicing of Easter Day, are three pages each bearing two pictures enclosed by a common frame: Christ's arrest and interrogation by Pilate, his scourging and descent from the Cross, his burial and manifestation to Mary Magdalene.

As in all pictures of this kind, the blue forms a sort of neutral background while the green serves partly to define the background and partly as a base. The two colours provide a very effective foundation for the pen-drawings in sepia and violet. The chromatic composition and technique of these drawings directly recall the contemporary Rhenish enamel-work from which they probably derived their inspiration.

Christ, bound to a slim pillar, is being scourged by two men armed with bunches of twigs. On the left stands a young man with his right hand poised to strike and his left raised in a gesture which is presumably expressive of mockery. Christ's loins are swathed in a cloth, and his body is already covered with wounds. He gazes sorrowfully at the ugly man on his left, who is also preparing to strike him. In contrast to the young man with the curly hair and elegant clothes, the second myrmidon is a caricature. He is depicted from behind, and the contours of his body are visible through his close-fitting robe. The extreme angle at which his head is set reveals his repulsive profile to full effect. Although his head is hairless save for one narrow curving lock, he affects a peculiar ringletted beard which leaves his chin bare. His mouth is opened in objurgation. Of the onlookers crowding in from the right, the first is probably Pilate, directing the scourging with raised hand.

If the upper picture tells of pain and brutality, the lower one is imbued with a spirit of quiet resignation. Christ's sufferings are over, and his corpse hangs limply in the arms of Nicodemus. His mother clasps his wounded right hand in hers, while his favourite disciple, John, holds his left. A diminutive hireling is still engaged in drawing the last nail from his foot. In the margin, half obscured by the frame, stands a weeping man. The 'Pietá' had still to become an artistic convention, but this picture illustrates the twelfth-century conception of the Descent from the Cross. All the figures are standing except that of Christ, which droops inertly. The participants' eyes are full of sorrow, and the look on Mary's face as she grasps her son's hand and arm is quite as expressive as in later Pietá portrayals, though far more restrained. The Cross is still depicted with a foot-bar to which the feet are nailed separately. The cross-beam and summit are cut at an oblique angle for reasons of perspective, a convention which persisted in Gothic portrayals of the Crucifixion.

Unfortunately, many of the magnificent early medieval manuscripts once owned by the monastery of St Peter's in Salzburg have since gone abroad. This antiphonary – the most precious item in the monastery's ancient library – was threatened with the same fate, but the Austrian government succeeded in purchasing it for the National Library in 1937.

III

EARLY GOTHIC ILLUMINATION
IN AUSTRIA AND GERMANY
THIRTEENTH-FOURTEENTH CENTURIES

Plate 12

PSALTER

253 leaves, 7½ × 5½ ins
2 circular pictures on each of the 12 Calendar pages
one full-page initial with miniatures, one ornamental page
9 historiated initials with ornamental borders and drolleries
Tyrol(?), *c.* 1270
Cod. 1898

PSALM INITIAL WITH ORNAMENTAL BORDER
FOL. 66ᵛ. ORIGINAL SIZE

Features typical of French figurative art occur, notably in the Calendar medallions, and the ornamental leaf- and branch-work and numerous figures point in the direction of Germany, but three miniatures, including the one reproduced here, are attributable to a master from Padua. Among other things, the school of painting to which he belonged embellished a sumptuous epistolary for Padua Cathedral with numerous miniatures. The scribe of this epistolary, which was completed in 1259, was a priest named Giovanni da Gaibana. The illuminators responsible for its decoration also decorated a number of other manuscripts which are now distributed among various libraries on both sides of the Atlantic. Some of these painters were also active in the archdiocese of Salzburg, where, apart from illuminating books, they carried out the murals in the Church of St Nicholas at Matrei in the East Tyrol.

In addition to Italian features, the style of this Paduan school of painting – sometimes known as the 'Gaibana School' – still betrays many signs of Byzantine influence. The face of King David in the present miniature is reminiscent of similar faces in Byzantine frescoes, but the painter of the group of animals was probably a German.

The book was produced at a Dominican friary. Evidence of this can be found not only in the Calendar but in a painting elsewhere in the manuscript, which shows a noblewoman receiving a book from the hands of a Dominican friar. The recipient cannot be identified with any certainty, but the psalter's place of origin is often assumed to be the Tyrol, which would account for its combination of French, German and Paduan stylistic features. If it did originate in the Tyrol, the lady in question is most likely to have been Adelheid, wife of Meinhard III von Görz, who died in 1278. A Dominican friary was founded at Bozen in 1274, so the book may possibly have been a thank-offering from the friary to its benefactress. It was acquired by the Imperial Court Library in 1783, after the dissolution of the Adeliges Damenstift at Hall in the Tyrol. The latter establishment had inherited it from one of the many Habsburg arch-duchesses who, after an eventful life on a European throne, spent a few meditative years in the tranquil atmosphere of the 'noblewomen's convent'.

Plate 13

MISSAL FOR AN ABBOT OF MONDSEE

81 leaves, 11⅛ × 7½ ins
One full-page miniature, 42 historiated initials in gold and colour
23 coloured initials
Written at Mondsee *c.* 1280 by Hartwig von Talmaizigen
Cod. 1827

CRUCIFIXION (FROM THE CANON)
FOL. 49ᵛ. ORIGINAL SIZE

relics. The ornamentation on the binding had disappeared by 1795, when the missal was incorporated in the Imperial Court Library after the dissolution of Mondsee.

Like the Liutold Gospels, produced in Mondsee in about the middle of the twelfth century (cf. p. 50), the Mondsee missal was signed by its scribe. The illumination may well have been carried out by someone else. The delicate execution of the numerous initials and the style and colouring of the Crucifixion suggest that they were the work of a professional book illuminator.

On the last page, complete with explanatory notes, are two hexameters embodying the name of the scribe, the manuscript's place of origin, and a curse on book-thieves:

'Scriptori requiem lector deposce perhennem
(Haertwico de Talmaizign).
Non uideat christum librum qui subtrahat istum
(Sancto michaheli in Maensee).'
(O Reader, request eternal peace for the scribe
[Hartwig of Talmaizigen].
May he not see Christ who removes this book
[from St Michael in Mondsee].)

Plate 14

GOSPEL LECTIONARY

134 leaves, 11⅜ × 7½ ins
14 full-page miniatures, numerous gold initials
Magdeburg area, latter half of the thirteenth century
Cod. Ser. N. 12,760

DEATH OF THE VIRGIN
FOL. 116ᵛ. ORIGINAL SIZE

The solemn splendour of the picture, whose treatment of architecture and physiognomy recalls Byzantine antecedents, is accentuated by a lavish use of gold. Most of the interior drapery falls in soft folds, but the garments culminate at the hem in the jagged indentations so characteristic of the latter half of the thirteenth century. The figures are boldly outlined, whereas the faces display a minimum of linear modelling. Of particular note are the universally 'Greek' noses of the various personages. The juxtaposition of colours is vigorous and rich in contrast, and much body-white has been used.

One clue to the book's date of origin is its omission of the Feast of Corpus Christi, which was generally introduced in 1274, so it must have originated prior to that year. As to its place of origin, two very similar manuscripts in Vienna are attributable to the Magdeburg area. Although this particular gospel lectionary mainly confines itself to listing the saints' days included in the universal Roman Calendar, it does make special mention of the Feast of St Maurice – yet another pointer to the Magdeburg area.

Acquired by the Imperial Family Entail Library during the nineteenth century, the manuscript passed to the Austrian National Library in 1920.

Plate 15

WOLFRAM VON ESCHENBACH AND ULRICH VON TÜRHEIM

'Willehalm' and 'Rennewart' (Sequel to the Willehalm)

351 leaves, 12⅜ × 8⅝ ins
107 miniatures, 15 illuminated initials
West Germany, c. 1320

SIEGE OF ORANGE BY THE HEATHENS
SCENE FROM THE RENNEWART
FOL. 221ᵛ. (DETAIL). ORIGINAL SIZE

IV

ILLUMINATION IN BOHEMIA AND MORAVIA
FOURTEENTH-FIFTEENTH CENTURIES

Plate 16

GOSPELS OF JOHANNES VON TROPPAU

189 leaves, 14¾ × 10⅛ ins
5 full-page miniatures, 4 ornamental pages embodying large initials
85 historiated initials
all pages of text adorned with frames and foliate corner-pieces
the entire text inscribed in gold with coloured majuscules
Written and illuminated in 1368 by Johannes von Troppau, Rural Dean of Landskron
Cod. 1182

LEGEND OF ST LUKE
FOL. 91ᵛ. ORIGINAL SIZE

The execution and general presentation of this book, which contains the text of the four Gospels, is unusually elaborate. The entire test is lettered in gold ink, each Gospel is prefaced by a full page illustrating the legend of the evangelist in question, and each of the pages opposite is devoted to a full-page initial. A fifth pictorial page – the last one in the book – portrays Christ in Judgement. The text is adorned with 85 pictorial initials, and every page of text is framed in colour and adorned with foliate corner-pieces.

This gospel-book is one of a group of manuscripts associated with the figure of Johannes von Neumarkt, Chancellor to Emperor Charles IV, who accompanied the emperor on his travels and so became familiar with Italy. He was a personal acquaintance of Petrarch, and, like him, venerated the written works of the ancient world. In emulation of the Italian humanists, he commissioned sumptuously illuminated manuscripts of which several have survived. As Pleban of Landskron, Johannes von Troppau must have been in close touch with the imperial chancellor, because Johannes von Neumarkt had owned Landskron since 1358 and thus held the right of presentation. It must therefore have been he who not only appointed Johannes von Troppau to the benefice of Landskron but also procured the artist his commission from Albrecht III, who had married a daughter of Emperor Charles IV in 1366.

The artists employed by the chancellor adopted a number of Italian stylistic features. Unlike the Bohemian and Moravian illuminators of the first half of the fourteenth century, painters active after the thirteen-fifties infused a great deal of life into the miniatures which they based on Italian models, abandoned two-dimensional representation in favour of spatial depth, and rejoiced in a wide-ranging palette. These features are observable in the work of Johannes von Troppau. Although this unique masterpiece is his only known work, his stylistic influence, possibly transmitted by pupils who studied under him, can still be observed in the early Wenzel manuscripts, just as, in general, the illuminators who worked for Johannes von Neumarkt also paved the way for the masterpieces which were produced for King Wenzel at Prague not long afterwards.

The gospel-book written for Albrecht III is one of the earliest manuscripts known to have been in Habsburg possession. In 1444, Frederick III inscribed the first page with his symbol of ownership – the letters A E I O V – and the date. In 1446 he ordered a splendid gilded silver cover for the book. This cover, the clasps of which are likewise engraved with the five vowels and the date, survives intact to this day.

Plate 17

GOLDEN BULL OF EMPEROR CHARLES IV

(copy)

80 leaves, 16½ × 17⅞ ins
One decorative page (page 1), 47 miniatures in text, 5 historiated initials
numerous initials in gold and colour
Prague, 1400
Cod. 338

Opening page
Fol. 1ʳ. Reduced

The love-knots and bathing-beauties which recur in all the manuscripts produced for King Wenzel, whether Bibles, astronomical treatises, poetical works, or – as here – legal statutes, pose considerable problems of interpretation.

The bathing-girls in the various Wenzel manuscripts are certainly not a punning allusion to the fact that Wenzel was aided in his escape from the citizens of Prague in 1393 by Susanna, a native of Baden ('baden' = bathe), since they already occur in a Wenzel manuscript completed in the year 1387. It is far more probable that the legend of Wenzel's release by a 'Baderin' named Susanna grew up as a result of the numerous illustrations in his books. The best explanation of the love-knots still seems to be that of Julius von Schlosser, who concluded seventy years ago that they symbolized Wenzel's love for his second wife, a Bavarian duke's daughter named Sophie who was also known by her second name Euphemia. Since the bathing-girls in Wenzel manuscripts are often depicted as crowned queens, and there is a frequent juxtaposition of crowned 'E' and crowned 'W', this would seem to be the obvious explanation. Bound to his queen by ties of deep affection, Wenzel embodied declarations of his love for her in all the books he commissioned. She not only sits beside him on the throne but performs all the intimate services expected of a dutiful wife, one of these – in the medieval view – being to wait on her husband in his bath.

The richly decorated title page was not done by the Master of the Golden Bull but by another artist known as the Hasenburg Master, after a missal which he illuminated for Sbinko von Hasenburg, Archbishop of Prague, in 1409. He was stylistically related to the Prague artists who collaborated on the decoration of King Wenzel's German Bible.

Like the majority of Wenzel's books, this copy of the Golden Bull passed via Emperor Sigismund, Wenzel's brother, and his daughter Elisabeth, wife of King Albrecht II, to Albrecht's cousin and successor, Emperor Frederick III. Frederick's son, Emperor Maximilian I, later brought this and many other books to Innsbruck. During the sixteenth century the Innsbruck manuscripts from Maximilian's estate were transferred to Schloss Ambras, where Archduke Ferdinand of the Tyrol had established his celebrated collection of *objets d'art* and curiosities. In 1665, after the Tyrolean Habsburgs had become extinct, most of the manuscripts were conveyed to Vienna by Peter Lambeck, the imperial librarian. This explains the library mark in Lambeck's handwriting at the head of the title-page of the Golden Bull: 'MS. Ambras 138'.

Plate 18

WENZEL BIBLE

6 volumes, 21⅛ × 14⅜ ins
Four are adorned with a total of 646 miniatures
and profuse marginal ornamentation
Prague, 1387–1400
Cod. 2759–2764

THE YOUNG SAMSON WITH HIS PARENTS; SAMSON RENDING A LION
FROM VOLUME II OF THE WENZEL BIBLE
FOL. 18ᵛ. EXCERPT, ORIGINAL SIZE

'Wenn wir uns hand gesetztet vor,   Dorumbe das dein kindel
Ouf sliessen deiner schrifte tor,   Die diser werlde swindel
Die manchem noch vorsperret sein,   Hat betoubet und verirret,
So das wir aus dem Latein   Und von dir verre gevirret,
Sie czu deutsche richten   Daraus helfe enpfahen
Und durch deinen namen tichten.   Und wider czu dir gahen...'

(For we have undertaken   that thy children,
to unlock the gates of thy texts,   whom the world's deceit
which are still closed to many,   hath confused and misled,
so that we translate them   and led far from thee,
from Latin into German,   shall receive aid therefrom
and write in thy name;   and return to thee once more...)

The production and, more especially, the lavish decoration of the book were undertaken at the king's command, as we are informed by a preamble which states that all who read it should render thanks to 'the high-born King Wenzlaw and his most illustrious Queen'.

Unfortunately, neither the text nor the artistic embellishment of the great translation was ever completed. Part of the Old and the whole of the New Testament are missing. The Bible, which is now divided into six volumes, comprises 1,213 leaves in all. The first volume contains 256 miniatures, together with a wealth of marginal ornaments. The second volume is fully illuminated, like the first. The third volume, which is only partly illuminated, contains 137 miniatures, one pen-drawing, and 53 spaces for further miniatures. The fourth and sixth volumes are devoid of artistic embellishment, but two passages in the fifth volume are adorned with a total of 19 miniatures. Wherever blank spaces have been left in the non-illuminated sections of the Bible, ink-written notes in the margin instruct the artist on how to fill them, so we are acquainted with the complete decorative scheme of the work.

Though uncompleted, the Bible kept several artists occupied for a considerable period. Since the preamble specifically mentions the queen, it can hardly have been started before 1389, the year in which Wenzel married his (second) wife. Wenzel's removal from the German throne (1400) seems to have heralded a slow decline in the activity of his atelier, so work on the Bible must have been largely confined to the decade 1390–1400.

Two sections of the Bible are inscribed, one at the beginning and one at the end, with names which may refer either to illuminators or scribes. The two names are 'Frana' and 'N. Kuthner'. Art historians have christened a series of artists after the various sections of the Bible on which they worked. There is, for example, the 'Master of the Seven Days', who illustrated the seven days of Creation in the first volume, the 'Exodus Master', who produced the miniatures for Exodus, and the 'Samson Master', who illustrated the story of Samson with scenes which include the two reproduced here. The Samson Master's figures were slender and graceful, their facial modelling carefully executed, and the direction of their gaze defined with invariable precision. He was fond of fashionable clothes and liked his drapery to hang in picturesque folds which helped to bring out the contrast in colour between superimposed layers of material (cf. Samson's mother). He was a young and talented artist who did not follow hackneyed exemplars slavishly but enjoyed giving free rein to his creative imagination.

Like the Golden Bull, the Wenzel Bible was acquired by the Habsburgs through the widow of King Albrecht II, went subsequently to Ambras, and entered the Imperial Court Library in 1665.

Plate 19

HASENBURG MISSAL

336 leaves, $9\frac{1}{2} \times 6\frac{3}{4}$ ins
One full-page miniature, 22 historiated initials
6 pictorial medallions in leaf-work, numerous initials
Written for Archbishop Sbinko von Hasenburg by Laurin von Klattau
Prague, 1409
Cod. 1844

EPIPHANY PAGE
ADORATION OF THE KINGS, WEDDING IN CANA, BAPTISM OF CHRIST
FOL. 26ᵛ. ORIGINAL SIZE

V
ILLUMINATION IN THE SERVICE OF
THE RULERS OF AUSTRIA
THIRTEENTH-FOURTEENTH CENTURIES

GULIELMUS DURANDUS
'Rationale' in German translation

330 leaves, 18¼ × 14¼ ins
9 pages lavishly adorned with leaf-work containing miniatures of various sizes
6 large and 134 smaller historiated initials, numerous smaller initials in gold and colour
Vienna, 1384–1406
Cod. 2765

CHRIST IN JUDGEMENT, WITH ANGELS
DUKE WILHELM OF AUSTRIA AND HIS WIFE JOANNA
FOL. 274ᵛ. REDUCED

and its two neighbours are occupied by angels whose function it is to transmit the prayers of the two suppliants to the altar. Their scrolls have also been left blank.

Kneeling at a wooden prie-dieu in the left-hand medallion is Duke Wilhelm of Austria, his upturned face captured in profile. He is wearing a blue fur-lined cloak modishly slashed at the hem, and his one visible foot is swathed in white. In front of the pew is an escutcheon bearing the arms of Austria. Standing at a discreet distance from the duke is his sword-bearer, clad in a blue coat with a blue-and-white sleeve and odd hose of the same two colours. Kneeling in the right-hand medallion, opposite her husband, is Joanna of Durazzo. The fact that she is identified by her coat of arms establishes Duke Wilhelm's identity beyond all doubt. In the absence of her coat of arms, he might have been assumed to be Albrecht IV. The duchess is kneeling at a prie-dieu similar to that of her husband. Visible beneath her robe, which is of rich red material lined with ermine, are the sleeves of a blue undergarment, and her head is covered with a close-fitting white coif. The duchess, too, is depicted in profile, and her hands are folded in the act of conveying her prayer, via the blank scroll, to the angel. In the background stands her maidservant, a figure in a blue undergarment almost wholly hidden from view by a dark cloak with red lining. Both sword-bearer and maidservant are so carefully painted that they may also have been portraits.

The large initial 'I' in pale red on a gold ground is almost overwhelmed by the sumptuous frame with its wealth of figurative decoration.

Nikolaus von Brünn is known to us partly from his activities at Klosterneuburg and partly from documentary records, notably the register of the Fraternity of St Christopher in Arlberg, which also bears his coat of arms. He was active in Vienna c. 1398–1430, and illuminated a series of books for Klosterneuburg as well as several works for the Austrian court. The 'Albrecht Master' (cf. p. 124) was one of his pupils.

Nikolaus favoured the use of sombre tones. The faces of his subjects are invariably executed in brownish shading, but their features are modelled with great precision. The portraits of his two patrons are particularly successful. The physiognomy of living people afforded the artist a greater opportunity to display his skill than saintly figures which had become crystallized by tradition. The colouring of the three large medallions in the lower margin possesses great charm as well. In the centre, the pale altar and its multi-coloured valance stand out three-dimensionally against a dark background. The figures of the duke in pale blue and the sword-bearer in another shade of the same colour provide an effective contrast to the wine-red background. In the right-hand medallion, the colour relationships have been reversed: the blue of the background accentuates the vivid red of the duchess's robe, and the sombre figure of the servant, with its faint touches of blue and red, forms a transitional link between the two colours.

Nikolaus von Brünn not only finished off this large work in accordance with contemporary style but succeeded, with complete homogeneity, in completing what other hands had started twenty years earlier. Richly embellished by no less than six different artists, the book is a fitting memorial to two decades of Viennese illumination. It was originally owned by the Viennese court, went to Innsbruck and Ambras at a later stage, and re-entered the Court Library in 1665.

Plate 21

LEGENDA AUREA (GOLDEN LEGEND)

287 leaves, 21¼ × 14⅛ ins
181 illuminated initials
Vienna, 1446–47
Cod. 326

INITIAL 'U' WITH ARMS, DEVICE AND MONOGRAM OF FREDERICK III
FOL. 1ᵛ. DETAIL, ORIGINAL SIZE

his notebook, so it is probable that the idea of using the five vowels as a magic symbol for the protection of his property was also acquired in the East. If this is so, people have credited the letters with far more significance than they originally possessed.

The arms, name and owner's mark on the very first page identify the book as Frederick III's personal property. The various artists who contributed to its embellishment are known to us through the medium of other manuscripts. One of them was Meister Michael, another Meister Martinus, whose principal work was the 'Trojan War', and the escutcheons are probably attributable to the Albrecht Master or one of his pupils.

Frederick III, though no aesthete, was a lover of precious things, and he placed books in this category. Having inherited large-scale books of high artistic quality from the estate of King Wenzel of Bohemia, he may well have been inspired to order similar books for himself, thereby affording artists at his court in Vienna an opportunity to practise their talents on a grand scale.

The big book remained in Habsburg keeping from the outset. Maximilian had it transferred to Innsbruck, together with many other manuscripts. From there it went first to Ambras and then, in 1665, to the Court Library in Vienna.

Plate 22

GUIDO DE COLUMNA
'History of the Destruction of Troy'

239 leaves, $14\frac{3}{4} \times 10\frac{3}{4}$ ins
9 initials, 334 miniatures of varying sizes
Vienna, *c.* 1445–50
Cod. 2773

PRIAM WELCOMING HELEN TO TROY
FOL. 68ᵛ. REDUCED

brow, and to whom he courteously commended himself with respectful words. And they came to the gate of the city, where a throng of people had assembled to celebrate their rejoicing and the magnificent spectacle with all manner of stringed instruments…')

Although the language is still Middle High German, it is comprehensible to the modern German reader. Its – to modern ears – naïve-sounding word formations and sentence constructions are closely followed by the pictorial representation of the scene, which is set in a vivid green meadow before the gates of Troy. Approaching from the left are Paris, Helen, and their entourage. Helen is mounted on a white horse, her gloved right hand grasping the red reins and her left hand a sort of sceptre. Over her red undergarment, whose sleeves are visible, she wears a long blue surcoat with gold embroidery and a white lining. The hair beneath her heavy crown, though abundant, is far less profuse than that of Paris. From what one can see of it, Paris's body looks very slender and disproportionately small in comparison with his face. This characteristic is common to all Martin's human figures.

In front of Helen's horse stands Priam, bidding her welcome. Since all that can be seen of him is his gold-embroidered mantle, the only clue to his identity is his crown. The grave old gentlemen in his train make a more majestic impression as they ride in from the right. Behind Priam is a servant, also seen from the rear, and another servant is engaged in helping Queen Helen to dismount. Two whippets, which the artist has depicted with the utmost delicacy, gambol about the horses' feet.

The straight road leads to a high, narrow gate behind which can be seen the wall of a wooden house. The other houses visible beyond the city walls are likewise built of wood, and the walls themselves are pierced by wide apertures with projecting sills. The spectators, crowded together behind them display little animation, unlike the two trumpeters on the left of the gate, who are blowing their instruments lustily with rounded cheeks.

This picture is typical of the master's style. He is fond of luminous colours applied in discreet gradations, and his figures are invariably constructed with great delicacy. Many of them appear to consist merely of a fashionable garment cut in fine cloth and a large, bewildered-looking face surmounted by a mass of curls. The broad facial expanses are modelled with a minimum of colours and are little able to express emotion. In this picture, the background has been filled with the houses and city walls of Troy. Blue sky and landscape can be seen in some of the other miniatures, but many still exhibit the gold backgrounds typical of the fourteenth century.

Though still nourished by tradition, this painter had made progress on his own account. None of the other artists active at the Austrian court was stylistically related to him. His figurative and landscape style hailed from the West, from the Middle or Upper Rhine, but he often collaborated with other Viennese illuminators on sizable works, e.g., the large Legendary for Frederick III (cf. p. 96) and another equally extensive devotional work for the same monarch.

The 'Destruction of Troy' was produced for the Austrian court. Maximilian must often have turned its pages and dipped into it, both as a young prince and later as emperor. A note on the fly-leaf informs us that it was for a time in the possession of Archduchess Magdalena, daughter of Emperor Ferdinand I, who founded the Noblewomen's Convent at Hall in 1569. The book may have been too worldly for her, because it passed into the collection of her brother, Ferdinand of the Tyrol, at Ambras, and from there, in 1665, into the Imperial Court Library at Vienna.

Plate 23

SCHOOL-BOOK OF MAXIMILIAN

22 leaves, 12 × 8⅝ ins
14 large initials, margins richly decorated with leaf-work and drolleries
Wiener Neustadt, *c.* 1467
Cod. Ser. N. 2617

Page of text with ornamental border
Fol. 8ʳ. Original size

three books. A prosperous patrician, Heuner occasionally made other financial sacrifices on the emperor's behalf.

Scribe and illuminator had to work on these books in close collaboration. It is probable that Heuner was familiar with the school-book for Ladislaus Postumus mentioned above, and that he ordered something similar. The scribe, whose name is known to us, was Wolfgang Spitzweck, a citizen of Wiener Neustadt, who worked in the Imperial Chancellery from 1442 onwards and later became clerk of his home town. He probably taught young Maximilian calligraphy as well. His lessons, coupled with the lettering in his school-books, made such a deep impression on Maximilian that in 1508, when he commissioned the printing of a new prayer-book, he submitted Spitzweck's school-book script as a model for the type face.

The name of the illuminator has never been identified, so he has been christened the 'School-book Master'. He produced other works apart from the three school-books, including a prayer-book for Maximilian's mother, Empress Leonora, and collaborated on yet another prayer-book with Ulrich Schreier (cf. p. 108).

The School-book Master was a pupil of the Albrecht Master. This is particularly apparent in his style of ornamentation, though his figures are far more animated than those of his more inhibited teacher. He instils a great deal of humour into his leaf-work and the creatures that clamber about in it, and his portrayals of human beings, even the solemn figures in Leonora's prayer-book, have an endearingly childlike quality.

The extremely tasteful presentation of this particular school-book extends to its binding, which has survived. The stout wooden covers are encased in deerskin, dyed red on the front and green on the back and stitched together along the spine. The brass fittings and clasps are also intact.

Unlike the two other school-books, which were transferred to Vienna from Schloss Ambras in 1665, this one did not enter the National Library until 1936, having previously formed part of the Ambras Collection in the Kunsthistorisches Museum.

Plate 24

BOOK OF HOURS

184 leaves, $5\frac{7}{8} \times 4\frac{3}{8}$ ins
21 full-page miniatures, 20 initials, many ornamental borders
Vienna, after 1470
Cod. Ser. N. 2599

ST MARGARET
FOL. 166ᵛ. ORIGINAL SIZE

This particular Book of Hours was not bound by Schreier, but it has some very fine filigree-work fittings in gilded silver, and the gilt edges are adorned with coloured floral designs.

The language of the book is Latin, but in the middle of the Latin liturgical texts in the first part is the only surviving text of an Easter hymn in German:

Krist ist erstanden
von der marter alle.
das sull wir alle fro sein,
christ soll unser trost sein,
kyrieleis.

Wer er nicht erstanden,
die welt die wer zergangen.
Sint daz er erstanden ist,
so loben wir vater jesu christ.
kyrieleis.

Maria du reine,
du hast so ser gewainet
umb unsern herren yesum christ
der all der welt ein troster ist,
kyrieleison.

Kyrieleison, christeleison, kyrieleison,
das sullen wir alle fro sein,
christ soll unser trost sein,
kyrieleison.

(Christ is arisen
of the martyrs all.
Then let us all rejoice,
let Christ be our consolation,
Kyrie eleison.

Were he not arisen
the world had passed away.
Since he is arisen
then let us praise Christ Jesu's father.
Kyrie eleison.

Mary, thou pure one,
thou hast wept so sorely
for our Lord Jesus Christ,
who is the consoler of all,
Kyrie eleison.

Kyrie eleison, Christe eleison, Kyrie eleison,
then let us all rejoice,
let Christ be our consolation,
Kyrie eleison.)

Plate 25

FIRST PRINTED GERMAN TRANSLATION OF THE BIBLE

2 volumes, paper; Volume I 195 leaves, Volume II 311 leaves, $15\frac{1}{2} \times 11\frac{1}{4}$ ins
Printed at Strasbourg by Johann Mentelin, 1466
Ornamental leaf-work on 19 pages, the majority with figures
numerous initials in gold and colour
South Germany or Tyrol, *c.* 1470
Incun. III. C. 6

JOB'S CHILDREN FEASTING
FROM VOLUME I OF THE MENTELIN BIBLE
FOL. 168ᵛ. DETAIL, REDUCED (ORIGINAL SIZE $7\frac{7}{8} \times 9$ ins)

Even though the illuminator cannot be identified with any other known painter of the period, related features can be found in the work of many of his contemporaries. One or two extraneous clues suggest that the book's artistic decoration may have originated in the Tyrol. Bound into the front of the Bible are twenty-nine handwritten sheets containing a detailed index of chapters and a list of the Epistles and Gospels to be read on feast-days throughout the Church Year. Entered against 13 May is a festival peculiar to Brixen in Austria and dedicated to its patron saint, Albinus. Yet another passage in the handwritten section indicates that the scribe was better acquainted with Austrian geography than the geography of the Bible, since he translated the First Epistle of Paul the Apostle to the Corinthians as 'Die erst epistel pauli zu den Kerntnern (Carinthians)'! Finally, suspended among the leaf-work at the foot of the first page of the printed text is the Austrian coat of arms.

Coupled with the entry referring to the Brixen festival, the Habsburg escutcheon renders it probable that the book was illuminated for Archduke Sigismund of the Tyrol.

The Mentelin Bible is one of the very few items in the present selection which were written or printed on paper as opposed to vellum. The watermark in the paper of the manuscript section is the so-called 'priest's hat', which only occurs in Italian papers, and papers of this type were in use both at Augsburg and in the Tyrol (Rattenberg) during the period 1469–76. Since the manuscript section is stylistically related to the illumination of the printed text, both would seem to hail from the Tyrol.

The art of illumination is, of course, intimately associated with the handwritten book, but in the period when the printed book was still in its infancy – hence the term 'incunabula' (literally, 'swaddling-clothes') applied to books printed prior to 1500 – printers vied with each other in producing volumes which resembled manuscripts as closely as possible. Except in cases where monochrome woodcuts were deemed sufficient, this entailed the adornment of particularly fine books with paintings, which had to be executed by hand as before. In the case of the present book – one of especial value since it was the first German Bible to be printed – the painter must have been commissioned either by someone who intended to present it to the archduke or by the archduke himself. We know that the Tyrolean court took an interest in printed books because one of the few verifiable owners of a 42-line Gutenberg Bible was Benedikt Wegmacher, priest of Merano and chief magistrate and chamberlain to Archduke Sigismund.

Plate 26

TYROLEAN FISHERY BOOK OF MAXIMILIAN I

60 leaves, 56 paper, 4 vellum, $12\frac{5}{8} \times 8\frac{3}{8}$ ins
2 complete armorial pages, 6 full-page landscapes, numerous calligraphic initials
Innsbruck, 1504
Cod. 7962

CATCHING CRAYFISH IN THE LIENZER KLAUSE
FOL. 48ᵛ. ORIGINAL SIZE

of the gorge and castle correspond to the actual topography. One gains the impression that the combination of picturesquely sited castle and overhanging cliffs was a product of the artist's imagination. The town in the background can only be Lienz, the only urban settlement in that part of Görz which had been inherited by Maximilian.

Flaring torches indicate that the catch is taking place by night. Lured out of their hiding-places by the torchlight, the crayfish are either caught by hand or prodded into nets with poles. They are then placed in flat baskets or shallow wooden tubs. On the bank stands a four-horse cart carrying a large cask into which the catch is emptied, and beside it are two fishermen's baskets. The man further down the road is standing beside a horse laden with two capacious panniers of the same shape as the smaller crayfish baskets. The cliffs rise steeply from the river on the left, and there is only just enough room for the road on the right. This is guarded by a defence-work with a narrow entrance. Beyond it, screened by a crenellated wall, the road leads to a bridge which debouches into the flat meadows in front of the town walls. The latter are interspersed with small towers, and visible behind them are the gables of a few houses. Perched on the overhanging cliff above the defence-work on the right is a castle with a projecting upper storey and vivid red roofs. This is linked to the outwork on the other side of the fosse by a wooden bridge.

The steep grassy slopes beyond the town are parcelled up by rows of trees. Behind them rise mountains, their peaks bathed in the same golden light that gilds the edges of the black clouds in the sky. The golden glow emanating from both sides of the castle rock suggests that the sun is rising, and the dense bushes and trees in front of the town are also lit with gold. Faced with the problem of depicting a night scene in which much detail would be obscured, the artist solved it by transferring the action to the hour before sunrise.

The painter of the Fishery Book was Jörg Kölderer, who came from Inzing in the Upper Inn Valley and had been in Maximilian's service since 1497. Kölderer continued to be so overwhelmed with commissions until Maximilian's death that he had to recruit several assistants to help him fulfil the emperor's manifold requirements. He remained in the imperial service until his own death in 1540. Apart from painting frescoes and miniatures, Kölderer worked as an architect and sculptor. He also produced sketches for Maximilian's large-scale graphic works, 'Triumphal Arch' and 'Triumphal Procession', which were later executed by Dürer and his associates, and lavished particular care on the pictures of Maximilian's cannon in his 'Arsenal Books'.

Kölderer was just the man to undertake the lively scenes in the Fishery Book, with their multiplicity of detail. Despite their damp and arduous duties, the fishermen are clad in bright colours, as are the two grooms. Here, as in other works, Kölderer took special delight in the luminous red of tiled roofs, and the design of the tower straddling the road and the lofty castle with its slanting roofs show him to have been an artist of architectural bent.

Though largely rooted in artistic tradition, the illustrations in the Fishery Book are already infused with the spirit which was introducing new modes of expression into Austria from Italy and the Netherlands. They are a faithful reflection of Maximilian's age and of the intellectual atmosphere in which he lived, just as Maximilian himself was a faithful guardian of the best traditions, but a man who constantly looked ahead, receptive to all the novel ideas of his day.

Plate 27

JAKOB MENNEL

'Der Zaiger'

Paper, 112 leaves, 11¾ × 8½ ins
21 full-page water-colours, 37 pages of genealogical drawings, also in water-colour
Freiburg im Breisgau, 1518
Cod. 7892

BUILDING A CASTLE
FOL. 10*ᵣ. ORIGINAL SIZE

It was universally accepted in Maximilian's day that the name Habsburg derived from 'haben', meaning 'have'. The *Zaiger* goes on to relate that the first Habsburgs were soon dislodged by their enemies. Much later, a new 'Habsburg' – the family seat of Maximilian's ancestors – was built not far from the original site in a land 'now' known as the 'aidgnosschaft' (confederation).

The genealogical fantasies of Maximilian's day strike us as incomprehensible now. All that really survives of this research, which was seriously intended at the time, is a large number of artistic master-pieces, including the bronze statues on Maximilian's tomb in Innsbruck. Also among the enduring relics of Mennel's research into the Habsburg family-tree are the pictures in the *Zaiger*.

In the centre of the miniature reproduced here is a conical hill partially overgrown with trees. Two labourers are carrying stones up the approach road to a crane manned by a third. The castle beyond it is almost complete except for the tower on the left, which is apparently being added to. In front of the blue hills in the background on the left rises a Gothic tower, and a carpenter can be seen at work in the fore-ground. His clothes are cut like those of a lansquenet, and he wears odd hose on either leg. The trees on the castle hill and in the left foreground are low and bushy. The only tall tree visible is the fir on the right, which has been stripped of its lower branches. Suspended from a red cord attached to one of the drooping upper branches is a small board obscured by white overpainting. Instead of a name or monogram, the board bears the artist's signature in the form of a device: a crossed flail and shepherd's crook. This artist's mark figures in other pictures as well but has almost invariably been overpainted at a later date. One miniature incorporates a self-portrait of the artist wearing a red cloak – a stalwart peasant of a man with dark hair and a black moustache.

The same artist illustrated other works by Mennel with pictures and genealogical trees. His paintings are not worked out in full detail, but their sketchy quality is allied with agreeable colouring. Although we do not know his name, his artistic origins are fairly easy to identify. Stylistically, he belongs to the Danube School as exemplified by Altdorfer and Wolf Huber. Another artist illustrated a biography of Emperor Frederick and Emperor Maximilian in a similar style somewhat earlier on. Although not identified with this painter, the 'Mennel Master' may conceivable have been apprenticed to him.

The presence of the *Zaiger* in the Imperial Court Library can be verified from the beginnings of the eighteenth century onwards.

Plate 28

HOURS OF ARCHDUKE ALBRECHT V OF AUSTRIA

222 leaves, 8¼ × 5⅝ ins
17 full-page miniatures, 16 historiated initials, more than 600 initials in gold and blue
Vienna, prior to 1437
Cod. 2722

CHRIST CARRYING THE CROSS
FOL. 80ᵛ, ORIGINAL SIZE

VI
ITALIAN ILLUMINATION
THIRTEENTH-SIXTEENTH CENTURIES

Plate 29

COLLECTION OF MEDICAL TEXTS

161 leaves, 10⅞ × 7⅜ ins
Over 400 illustrations of which one or more on each page
Italy, first half of the thirteenth century. Copy of a Late Antique original
Cod. 93

TREATMENT FOR GOUT
FROM A MEDICAL WORK BY ANTONIUS MUSA
FOL. 9ᵛ. ORIGINAL SIZE

and symbolic representations; and, secondly, illustrations of herbs and animals, of the methods to be adopted when preparing and administering medicaments, and of doctors and patients giving and undergoing various forms of medical treatment. The picture reproduced here belongs to the latter group. The outlines of the figures are mostly pen-drawn. Faces, hands and feet are lightly modelled in brown in addition to being picked out in ink. Clothing and utensils are painted in body-colours, shadows applied in darker gradations of the same. The artist favours unbroken planes of vivid colour, and his independence of Antique models is apparent in many details, notably the treatment of heads and drapery. What chiefly points to Italy as the land of origin is the script. The ink-drawings, which are later than the miniatures, belong stylistically to the Italian art of the second half of the thirteenth century. This suggests that the manuscript itself originated at about the middle of the same century. Since Salerno was the main centre of medical research in Europe at the time, it is probable that copies of medical text-books were also produced there. In view of the brisk demand for such works, they were often copied many times over. Many of these copies succumbed to wear and tear or were lost, but several have survived to this day.

This particular manuscript has been in the Imperial Court Library from the late eighteenth century onwards.

Plate 30

PORCIUS AZO

'Commentary on the first five books of the Codex Justiniani'

152 leaves, $16\frac{1}{2} \times 8\frac{3}{8}$ ins
Several large miniatures and historiated initials
361 small initials containing half-length miniatures
Bologna, first half of the fourteenth century
Cod. 2256

BETROTHAL SCENE; KNIGHT SLAYING DRAGON
FOL. 123^V. EXCERPT, ORIGINAL SIZE

proceeding devoid of religious significance. In the centre stands the lawyer, dressed in a pale green robe and a violet gown with a fur lining and fur collar. His left hand is concealed beneath his gown and his right hand extended towards the prospective husband. Stationed behind the latter, with one hand laid protectively on his shoulder, is a grown man. This is evidently an act of betrothal between minors, because the prospective bride, who is escorted by two women, looks quite as young as her fiancé. She stands there serenely with both hands hidden beneath her red overgarment, eyes fixed on the tiny ring in the boy's right hand.

In fact, the significance of the scene is explained by the accompanying text. It depicts the payment of the 'arrha' or earnest-money which customarily changed hands as a pledge of good faith. The three adults escorting and chaperoning the two young people are probably 'prosenetici', or matchmakers, who were entitled to a fee for their services.

The illuminator did not confine himself to one functional miniature. As on other pages, the columns of text are separated by an ornamental 'creeper' divided into segments by leaves, knots, and loops. A third of the way down it stands a man in a scarlet robe and blue cloak, holding a book in his hands and looking over his shoulder at the betrothal scene.

At the foot, where the ornamental creeper terminates in two frond-like branches, the illuminator abruptly deserts the world of dry legal reality and gives witty and elegant expression to his personal views on the subject of betrothals: the implication is that, sooner or later, they involve a man in armed combat with a dragon! Attired in brown leggings, a short pink tunic, blue harness trimmed with brown, chain-mail cap and pointed helmet, a knight armed with spear and shield is transfixing the slender neck of an olive-green dragon.

We do not know the artist's name, but the manuscript is one of those Bolognese School works in which French and Byzantine influences combined to form a new, typically Italian style. It is distinguished not only by its extremely careful execution but also by its wealth of embellishment. In addition to several fairly large miniatures and historiated initials, it embodies no fewer than 361 small initials with short ornamental borders and half-length miniatures in their interior. The painter's palette is typical of Bolognese manuscripts of the first half of the fourteenth century. He employs rich, heavy colours, and favours the use of green when depicting human physiognomy.

This manuscript belonged to the library of Prince Eugene of Savoy during the eighteenth century. It was acquired by the Imperial Court Library in 1738, two years after his death.

Plate 31

TACUINUM SANITATIS

109 leaves, $13\frac{1}{4} \times 9$ ins
206 miniatures
Northern Italy (Verona?), late fourteenth century
Cod. Ser. N. 2644

Equitatio (Horsemanship)
Fol. 102[r]. Original size

whereas the airy loggia annexed to the palace reposes on Gothic arches and is surmounted by Gothic gables. A woman has just ascended the steps after picking some roses in the garden.

The two horses are rather sturdily built, especially the dapple-grey in the foreground, but the latter is equipped with rich trappings and a carefully painted saddlecloth which sets off the green costume of its rider to advantage. His tight-fitting hose culminate in long piked toes. Both horsemen are allowing their beasts to trot peacefully along while they converse with one another. The tufts of grass on the ground indicate that they are riding through a meadow. Across the foot of the picture runs a jagged rocky border which recalls earlier Italian paintings of the Trecento.

Everyone used to ascribe the illustrations in this Tacuinum to the Verona-Padua area, but modern authorities on Italian art consider Lombardy to be the more likely place of origin. Debate on the subject is not yet closed, however. At least some of the pictures, including the one reproduced here, have been attributed to the brothers Franco and Filippolo de 'Veris, who painted the frescoes on the exterior wall of a small church at Campione (near Como) in the year 1400. Another theory is that the pictures were produced by a Lombardic illuminator of Giovannino de 'Grassi's circle.

The main argument in favour of the Verona attribution is a superficial one, namely, that there is a detailed reproduction of the arms of the Cerruti, a Veronese family, at the beginning of the book. Very early in its career, the 'Tacuinum' came into the possession of Georg von Lichtenstein, Bishop of Trento from 1390 to 1419, and his arms were entered on the hitherto blank fly-leaf.

The book was re-bound during the sixteenth century, probably when it entered Archduke Ferdinand's collection at Ambras. Ferdinand's first wife, the Augsburg noblewoman Philippine Welserin, took a keen interest in home-made remedies and left behind several collections of recipes, some for medicaments and others for the preparation of tasty roasts and cakes.

The 'Tacuinum', whose wealth of artistic decoration had made it a frequent object of study over the years, was not transferred from the Kunsthistorisches Museum to the National Library until 1936.

Plate 32

PETRARCH

'Triumphs'

54 leaves, 8⅜ × 5¼ ins
7 miniatures with ornamental frames, 15 initials
School of Verona, 1459
Cod. 2649

TRIUMPH OF VIRTUE
FOL. 35ᵛ. ORIGINAL SIZE

nensis' as the scribe. (He was probably the illuminator as well.) Since another very similar copy of the same work, now in Dresden, was completed by the same scribe at Pesaro on 29 April 1460, it is likely that the present copy also originated at Pesaro. The work contains a total of seven miniatures adorned with sumptuous ornamental borders, together with numerous initials of various sizes. The opening and concluding passages of each book are written in gold ink.

Painstaking though the illuminator was, his figurative work and crowd scenes are often maladroit. His human figures betray a dependence on Pisanello, the greatest Veronese master of the first half of the century, but his technique is inferior. The ornamental borders are far more successful than the miniatures inside them. Convoluted spirals of white leaf- and branch-work were a common feature throughout Italy, but the contrast between the sturdy main stems and the dainty leaf-tipped tendrils is typical of the Italian North. The illuminator was adept in spinning his rich tracery of lines into separate motifs disposed at rhythmical intervals.

The allegorical approach of this carefully written and illuminated work stimulated Renaissance art in a number of ways. Petrarch (1304–74) was one of the first humanists, both in period and status. He cherished the deepest respect for the writers of antiquity and imitated their classical Latin, but he was also, in company with Dante and Boccaccio, one of the fathers of literary Italian. His Italian works include the *Trionfi* ('Triumphs'), begun in 1357 and written, like Dante's *Divina Commedia*, in terza rima. This poem extols the triumph of various forces in an allegorical manner, after the fashion of a triumph celebrated by a Roman general.

These allegories provided Renaissance painters with a welcome source of material. 'Triumphs' of this kind were painted not only by illuminators but by other artists, who embodied them in frescoes and panel-paintings. The 'Dance of Death' had been treated in similar fashion before Petrarch's day, but it was characteristic of the humanist mentality that the palms of victory, hitherto awarded to death alone, should now be conferred upon the forces of life.

We do not know for whom the present manuscript was originally written and illuminated. It remained in Italy, presumably, because in 1725 it was in the possession of Cardinal Alessandro Albani, who later (1761) became Prefect of the Vatican Library. The cardinal presented the book to Prince Eugene of Savoy, accompanying it with a letter written in Rome and dated 7 July 1725. It was acquired by the Imperial Court Library in 1738, with the rest of Prince Eugene's collection.

AENEAS SILVIUS PICCOLOMINI (POPE PIUS II)

'On Education'

74 leaves, $8\frac{1}{2} \times 5\frac{7}{8}$ ins
Armorial page consisting of escutcheons in an ornamental frame
3 decorative borders, numerous initials
Written and illuminated in Rome in 1466
Cod. Ser. N. 4643

ARMORIAL PAGE
FOL. 1ᵛ. ORIGINAL SIZE

copy originally in his possession. He did not do so straight away, however, and his library sustained damage during the disorders which later broke out in Vienna. Time passed, and Hinderbach was made Bishop of Trento. Eventually, while visiting Rome in 1466, he remembered the promise he had made to the empress and Jakob Fladnitzer, Rector of Vienna's Bürgerschule and Prince Maximilian's erstwhile tutor. Seeking a substitute for his lost copy, he discovered that the Cardinal of Sienna, a nephew of the late Pope, was in possession of Piccolomini's original manuscript, complete with corrections and additions. Hinderbach commissioned an experienced scribe to copy it, preface it with his dedicatory letter, and adorn it with suitable miniatures. The letter of dedication, dated 14 May 1466, suggested that the prince should add the booklet to his personal possessions, his other books, weapons and toys. When he grew a little older, the sight of the handsome volume might possibly put him in mind of the donor and of the church of Trento.

Piccolomini's treatise was not designed to introduce any radical changes into Maximilian's elementary schooling, which followed the contemporary pattern, but merely to augment it by suggesting linguistic exercises and contests which accorded with the high value attached by humanists to the art of rhetoric. Although drafted in the mid-'forties as an educational programme for Ladislaus (b. 1440), son of Albrecht II, Piccolomini's curriculum was just as applicable in 1466 to the education of Maximilian (b. 1459). Nevertheless, it is doubtful if either of the two people for whom the work was copied in Rome ever made use of it: Jakob Fladnitzer, Maximilian's first tutor, died in the same year, and Empress Leonora in 1467.

The book's interior is matched by its handsome exterior. The brown leather cover is adorned, back and front, with broad borders of strap-work composed of small blocked impressions, and the star-shaped centre-piece is decorated with similar impressions. Coloured discs are punched into the leather between the blocked strap-work. The book was originally secured by four pairs of green straps, two on the fore-edge and one each at the head and foot, but nothing remains of these except the ends affixed beneath the leather binding.

Like Maximilian's other school-books, this one must have remained in his possession for some time. Whether he gave it away to a close friend, as he often did with his books, or whether it left his neglected library at a later stage, it remained lost from view until 1931, when it turned up at a London dealer's and was acquired for the Austrian National Library.

Plate 34

ROMAN BREVIARY

2 volumes printed on vellum, Venice 1481. 468 leaves in all, 6¼ × 4 ins
The first volume contains 3 ornamental pages, 3 full-page miniatures
10 decorative borders, 11 initials, one of them historiated
Inc. 3H.64/1

Vision of the Prophet Isaiah
Vol. I, fol. 9ᵛ. Original size

the printer used vellum of peculiarly fine quality. Again, few printed books were illuminated by first-class painters. Many incunabula contained hand-painted initials, it is true, but these paintings were – at best – neat workmanlike jobs rather than works of art in their own right. Incunabula with figurative decoration were produced throughout Europe, but only for particularly demanding clients who wished their printed books to receive the same form of embellishment as a manuscript. Indeed, it was the joint aim of printer and illuminator to make their books as handsome as any handwritten volume.

This particular book was commissioned by one of the Barozzi, a noble Venetian family whose coat of arms appears throughout but was later overpainted in white.

During the eighteenth century, both volumes were re-bound in a mosaic of dyed leather adorned with hand-gilding. The craftsman responsible for these sumptuous new covers was Nicolas Padeloup, book-binder to Gaston, Duke of Orleans. In 1720 the books were in the possession of Prince Eugene of Savoy's Adjutant-General, Baron von Hohendorf, whose library was acquired in the same year by Emperor Charles VI.

Plate 35

TACITUS

'Annals, Histories, Germania'

236 leaves, 12¾ × 8¾ ins
One ornamental frame with miniature and escutcheon, several initials
Naples, *c.* 1485
Cod. 49

ORNAMENTAL FRAME WITH BUST OF TACITUS AND BEGINNING OF BOOK 11 OF THE ANNALS
FOL. 2ᵛ. SLIGHTLY REDUCED

The text tells of events in 47 BC, when Rome was ruled by Emperor Claudius. The eleventh book opens with a description of a plot against a certain Valerius Asiaticus, who was indicted before the emperor on a trumped-up charge.

The scribe of this manuscript, which was written in painstaking classical book-script, was probably the Neapolitan calligrapher Joannes Rainaldus Mennius, who produced other gorgeously illuminated manuscripts for the court of Naples. The illuminator may have been Christophoro Majorana, a Neapolitan who often embodied architectural constructions in his miniatures.

The original binding – red maroquin with gilded strap-work borders – has survived. The gilt edges are decorated with punched rosettes.

An inscription inside the front cover suggests that this superbly illuminated book was undertaken originally for Cardinal Giovanni d'Aragona, a son of King Ferdinand I of Naples. Later, possibly after the cardinal's death (1485), it was completed for the king, whose coat of arms adorns the front page.

This manuscript was one of several acquired in Naples in 1563 by Johannes Sambucus (d. 1584), the imperial historiographer, who inscribed his name and the date of purchase on the first page of the text. Part of Sambucus' library came into the Imperial Court Library during his lifetime and the remainder was purchased by Blotius, the imperial librarian, in 1587. One of Blotius' successors, Peter Lambeck (1663–80), entered the Court Library's mark of ownership beneath that of Sambucus.

Plate 36

ARISTOTLE

'Nicomachean Ethics'

90 folios, 16⅝ × 11¼ ins
10 full-page miniatures
Abruzzi, *c.* 1500
Cod. Vindob. Phil. graec. 4

ALLEGORY OF PRUDENCE AND UNDERSTANDING
BELOW, SCENES FROM THE ODYSSEY: POLYPHEMUS AND THE SIRENS
INTRODUCTORY PICTURE TO BOOK 6 OF THE NICOMACHEAN ETHICS
FOL. 45ᵛ. REDUCED

woman and the body of a lion. The significance of this picture has never been determined beyond doubt, but the interpretation put forward in the seventeenth century by Peter Lambeck, the court librarian, seems plausible enough. According to this, the girl personifies man's natural craving for knowledge and the sphinx symbolizes the human soul, which comprises a rational element, hence the human head – and an irrational element – hence the lion's body. On the other hand, the sphinx may be a symbol of the enigmatic, a symbol of deliberation and divination, mental activities which demand sagacity and discernment. Classic examples of this are provided by Odysseus, whose cunning is illustrated by three episodes from his wanderings. Bands of laurel-leaves not only enclose the entire page but also separate the upper picture and the panel of text from the three scenes devoted to the Odyssey.

In the centre is a vista of open sea bounded in the far distance by blue mountains and a yellow-tinged horizon. The scene in the foreground shows Odysseus evading the lure of the sirens, who have already emerged from the fishy depths with their lips parted in song. Odysseus himself stands in the waist of the largest ship, clad in full armour. His companions have lashed him to the mast and have fallen asleep.

The scene on the left depicts the blinding of Polyphemus as he lies outside his cave with a half-empty wine-skin on the ground beside him. Odysseus is thrusting a heated stick into the giant's single eye with both hands while his three bound companions stand idly by.

The right-hand scene illustrates Odysseus' escape from the now blinded Polyphemus. The giant stands erect before the cave with his eye-socket still oozing blood, feeling the backs of his sheep as they emerge, one by one, to ensure that none of his enemies manages to sneak out with them. Having tied himself to a sheep's belly with rope, Odysseus succeeds in evading the giant's groping fingers.

The entire page is a splendid illustration of the humanists' delight in allegories and scenes from the world of classical antiquity. The other nine pictorial pages in this book, which represents one of the most interesting relics of Italian Renaissance book illumination, come from the same world of ideas.

An explanation of the artist's signature referred to previously appears on the last of the ten pictorial pages, the lower margin of which bears the inscription: REGINALDVS PIRAMVS MONOPOLITANVS LIBRVM HVNC PICTVRIS DECORAVIT MIRIFICE (Reginaldus Piramus of Monopoli adorned this book with paintings in a wondrous manner). This seems to indicate that the letters 'R' and 'F' stand for 'Reginaldus fecit'. (The town of Monopoli, near Bari is situated in an area where Duke Andrea Matteo once owned estates.)

The scribe of the manuscript was probably Angelos Konstantinos, a calligrapher known to have produced several other manuscripts in Greek.

The book was purchased in Naples *c.* 1563 by Johannes Sambucus, the imperial historiographer, and presented in the same year to Maximilian, King of Bohemia and later Emperor Maximilian II.

Plate 37

MISSAL

177 leaves, $15\frac{3}{4} \times 10\frac{7}{8}$ ins
One full-page miniature, 23 historiated initials, 25 pages with full ornamental frames
ornamental borders on almost all other pages, numerous initials of various sizes
Northern Italy, *c.* 1510
Cod. Ser. N. 2843

NATIVITY SCENE
FOL. 4r. REDUCED. ORIGINAL SIZE (EXCLUDING VELLUM BORDER): $14\frac{5}{8} \times 10\frac{1}{4}$ ins

water's edge is a mountain crowned by a castle. In the middle distance, between trees with gold-speckled foliage, can be seen the massive towers and blue roofs of another town. The left-hand side of the picture is devoted to an expanse of luxuriant green grassland, a stony path, and a blue stream. The blue of the sky increases in intensity towards the top of the picture. The angels floating on the clouds are singing *Gloria in excelsis* and proclaiming the birth of Jesus to the solitary shepherd who stands – a much larger figure than the laws of perspective would normally permit – gazing up to heaven. The shepherd on the extreme left is completely engrossed in the music of his bagpipe.

This miniature is one of the '*c.* 1520' works which represent the swansong of Italian book-painting, but it demonstrates that even this terminal phase could give birth to masterpieces of the finest quality.

The missal is preserved in the Austrian National Library on permanent loan from the heirs of A. Rothschild.

Plate 38

HOURS OF QUEEN JOANNA I OF NAPLES

348 leaves, 6⅞ × 5 ins
All Calendar pages adorned with signs of the zodiac and monthly occupations
20 full-page and 22 smaller miniatures, 14 large initials, some historiated
Naples, between 1346 and 1362
Cod. 1921

BEHEADING OF JOHN THE BAPTIST
FOL. 211ʳ. ORIGINAL SIZE

VII

ILLUMINATION IN FRANCE AND ENGLAND
THIRTEENTH-FIFTEENTH CENTURIES

Plate 39

BIBLE MORALISÉE

130 leaves, 13⅜ × 10¼ ins
One full-page miniature, 8 pictorial medallions on each
of the remaining 129 leaves (painted one side only)
1,032 miniatures in all
Champagne (Rheims?), mid-thirteenth century
Cod. 2554

STORY OF ENOCH AND NOAH'S ARK
FOL. 3ʳ. REDUCED

stands Christ with a bishop on his right and a monk on his left. The figures behind the monk are partially obscured, and the Mother of God, though referred to in the text, is nowhere to be seen.

The story of the Ark continues in the third pair of medallions. The ship's structure remains the same, but changes have occurred in the distribution of its passengers, human and animal. Noah now sits alone in the first compartment. The accompanying text tells of the four birds he dispatched: first, a dove, which returned; then another dove, which returned with its feet wet because the earth had not yet dried out; then a raven, which found some carrion somewhere and did not return at all; and, finally, a third dove, which flew back with an olive-branch in its beak. All four creatures are depicted here: at the top, a dove setting forth; below it, the dove with the olive-branch; perched on the gunwale facing Noah, a dove with nothing in its beak; and beneath the Ark, which is still floating in green water, a large bird devouring something on terra firma.

The interpretation of this picture is sternly moral in tone. Noah is the good prelate who constantly exhorts his flock to prayer. The first dove (which returned home at once) is the good monk who never ventures from the monastery and dies there. He can be seen lying supine behind the abbot with his soul soaring heavenwards in the guise of a naked man. The two other doves, which returned after a long absence, symbolize good monks who come back to the monastery after spending time in the outside world. The one in the red habit stands with hands outspread, while the other, dressed in a blue habit, hands the abbot a rod in readiness to undergo chastisement. Finally, the raven symbolizes the bad monk who is for ever lingering over the carrion of this world. The earthly realm, separated from the monastic realm by a flimsy architectural construction, is represented by a laden table at which the bad monk sits and drinks while a shifty-looking young man hands him a large purse of money.

The last two medallions refer to the exodus from the Ark. Above, the human passengers step ashore by way of a slanting plank while the birds take wing and the four-legged beasts prepare to disembark two by two. On the right, Noah and his wife stand before a white-draped altar with their hands raised towards God, who blesses them from the small window above and to the right.

The final scene interprets Noah's prayer of thanksgiving and sets the pattern for similar prayers offered up by those who trust in God to deliver them from all dangers, whether by land or water. The medallion depicts three figures, one menaced by predatory beasts on dry land, the second standing erect aboard ship, and the third in the process of being devoured by a monstrous fish. All three have raised their hands to God, who once again gestures in benediction from above.

Not all the foregoing interpretations of Biblical scenes accord with modern religious sentiments and ideas. The thirteenth century – the century of scholasticism – derived greater satisfaction from religious allegories than we do today. Not very many people can have had a chance to examine these richly illuminated books, nor can we tell what effect the few copies of the *Bible Moralisée* had upon those who first read them and studied their thousands of miniatures. To the modern observer, however, they represent a pictorial encyclopedia of secular and religious life in thirteenth-century France.

The Imperial Court Library inherited this superb manuscript from the Adeliges Damenstift at Hall in the Tyrol in 1783.

Plate 40

PSALTER (AND PICTURE-BIBLE)

204 leaves, 6⅞ × 5¼ ins
14 pictorial pages each with 6 Biblical scenes
Calendar with zodiacal signs and monthly occupations
10 full-page psalm initials
textual pages ornamented with numerous small initials
and line-fillings
North-East France, third quarter of the thirteenth century
Cod. Ser. N. 2611

PSALM INITIAL 'D' CONTAINING SCENES FROM THE LIFE OF KING DAVID
FOL. 57ᵛ. ORIGINAL SIZE

Comparison with other works indicates that this lavishly illuminated psalter originated in Northeast France rather than Paris. It may have been produced for a Bohemian client, since the feast of St Wenceslaus appears in red in the Calendar. So brisk was the demand for devotional works of this type in France between the second half of the thirteenth and the beginning of the sixteenth century that ateliers churned them out by rote. This particular specimen far surpasses the purely routine, however, both in quality of execution and iconographic originality.

The psalter is further enhanced by a fourteen-page picture-Bible bound in at the front. Each page carries six pictorial medallions. Of the eighty-four scenes depicted, sixty refer to Genesis from the Creation to the death of Jacob, and twenty-four to the New Testament from the Annunciation to the Last Judgement. This picture-Bible contains no written text. The pictures were intended to attract the eye and tell their own story.

The original binding no longer exists, but during the sixteenth century the book was given a new binding worthy of its sumptuous interior. The red leather cases are entirely sheathed in a single layer of velvet and two layers of silk trimmed at the edges with silver braid. The front and back covers are each fitted with five rosettes of gilded silver.

The psalter was in the Kunstkammer at Schloss Ambras during the sixteenth century. In 1806, in company with other books, it was acquired by Vienna's Kunsthistorische Sammlungen, and in 1936 by the Austrian National Library.

Plate 41

BOHUN PSALTER

160 leaves, 11⅛ × 7½ ins
Calendar adorned with miniatures depicting signs of the zodiac and monthly occupations
6 large historiated initials with ornamental borders
over 200 smaller historiated initials, more than 3000 non-historiated initials
coloured line-fillings on every page
South of England, *c.* 1370
Cod. 1826*

Last Judgement
Fol. 141ʳ. Original size

tendrils with coloured leaves and, in the central loop, the royal arms of England. They are, in fact, the arms which Edward III (1312–77) adopted in 1340, after winning major successes in France during the early stages of the Hundred Years' War. The first and fourth quarters of the escutcheon bear the arms of France, the second and third those of England.

The broad gold ornamental border with which the two ramifications of the initial merge on the left is extended along the upper edge by a double gold line with an ornamental leaf at its tip. Here, the double line divides, sending a thin tendril down the right-hand side of the page to join a similar tendril which rises to meet it from the lower border. Both tendrils bear small gold leaves. On the left, beneath the medallion depicting the damned, the ornamental border tapers in two stages before swelling again to form a thick knot with a dragon partly composed of vegetation growing out of it. Suspended beneath the lion's head in the centre of the narrow lower border, is another representation of the royal coat of arms.

The small initials at the beginning of verses are purely ornamental, but the line-fillings are half vegetable, half animal. Like the schematic gold leaves, these minor decorative features were probably carried out by assistants who seldom if ever helped to execute historiated initials.

It took a whole team of illuminators and scribes quite some time to produce a book as lavishly illuminated as this one, yet Humphrey de Bohun commissioned several works of this type within the space of a few years. Careful examination of the miniatures helps one to differentiate between the individual artists who collaborated on them, but their styles harmonize to such an extent that each work might have come from a single mould.

Humphrey de Bohun was an English forerunner of the great Continental bibliophiles who were soon to accumulate libraries containing exquisite masterpieces of the book illuminator's art – Jean Duc de Berry (d. 1416) in France and King Wenzel IV (d. 1419) in Bohemia. Like their handwritten books, the Bohun manuscripts did not remain together for long, and they are now distributed among various libraries and countries. Having been in the possession of one Johann Stanislaus Roznicki during the seventeenth century, Vienna's Bohun manuscript turned up at a Viennese dealer's in 1852 and was acquired by the Imperial Court Library for two hundred gulden.

Plate 42

ROMAN DE LA ROSE

175 leaves, 11¾ × 8⅜ ins
65 miniatures, 61 initials with ornamental borders, several ornamental frames
Paris, *c.* 1370–1375
Cod. 2592

Two miniatures depicting the Lover and the God of Love
Fol. 15ᵛ. Original size

The second miniature bears the superscription 'Comment il dieu d'amours ferme a l'amant le coste a la clef' (How the God of Love locks the Lover's side with a key). The God of Love, now clad in a filmy pink overgarment and an undergarment of the same luminous colour as his wings, is silhouetted against a blue background adorned with feathery spirals of gold-leaf work. He is bending forward in the act of locking the Lover's heart with the large key in his right hand. The Lover gazes anxiously at the deity with his left hand raised. His costume – lilac tunic, green hood and pink hose – differs from that of the first picture, and his face has changed too. The beardless youth has become a man, and now wears a fair beard of fashionable cut. Alterations in physiognomy often occur in these pictures, probably because they were painted by several different illuminators whose stylistic schooling was so homogeneous that only iconographic divergencies enable one to differentiate between their work.

In both miniatures, the Lover's costume consists of a close-fitting tunic which reaches to the middle of the thigh and is gathered at the waist. The sword-belt hangs low on his hips, and the hood covering his shoulders extends down his back as far as the belt. Like other details of fashion, the fair beard and long piked shoes belong to the reign of Charles V of France (1364–80).

The numerous Roman de la Rose manuscripts differ greatly, both in quality and style. In the present example, both text and miniatures were executed with the utmost care. It is impossible to identify the man who commissioned it, although a historiated initial in the final section of the book depicts him kneeling before the Trinity in a tabard. (Despite the frivolous nature of the amatory allegories in the Roman de la Rose, both authors and readers accepted the conventions of Christianity as a matter of course.) He must have been close to the king, because only courtiers had sufficient good taste and material resources to enable them to commission books for their libraries from artists of the first rank.

This particular manuscript was acquired in France by Baron von Hohendorf, Adjutant-General to Prince Eugene of Savoy. It went to the Imperial Court Library in 1720, together with his other books.

Plate 43

BOOK OF HOURS

354 leaves, 6⅛ × 4¼ ins
29 miniatures of half-text depth, 24 historiated initials, all pages adorned with foliage
Southeast France(?), late fourteenth century
Cod. Ser. N. 9450

SS John the Baptist, John the Evangelist and James
Fol. 44ʳ. Original size

of the borders enclosing miniature and text. Issuing from these borders, with their patterns of blue and reddish-brown, are tendrils bearing spiky leaves in gold, red, and blue. The upper border takes the form of two hybrid creatures composed of ornamental leaf-work, dragons' feet and wings, and grotesque masks.

Variations on the decorative theme of this page occur throughout the book. In later examples of French book illumination, the conventional cusped foliage is carried out in a purely routine manner, as though stencilled. The ornaments in this book, though done by a practised hand, are freely executed. The artist was not only at liberty to exercise his imagination but gave it free rein throughout the book.

Both miniatures and ornaments are related in style to the work of the masters active at the French court during the closing decades of the fourteenth century, whereas the Calendar and the pictures of the saints mentioned individually in prayers point to the Avignon area of Southeast France.

The book was still in Paris when put up for auction in 1883. It later went to a private collection in Vienna, where it remained until the Austrian National Library acquired it from a trade source in 1959.

Plate 44

ROMANCE OF TRISTAN AND THE ROUND TABLE

492 leaves, 18¾ × 13¼ ins
144 miniatures of column-width, numerous initials of various sizes, many ornamental borders
Paris, second decade of the fifteenth century
Cod. 2537

TRISTAN'S MARRIAGE TO ISEULT OF THE WHITE HAND
FOL. 71ʳ. DETAIL, ORIGINAL SIZE

coloured flowers. Tristan has taken Iseult's left hand in his right. His own left hand is raised, whereas Iseult's disengaged hand reposes on her left forearm. On the right, behind Iseult, is the figure of her royal father escorted by Tristan's faithful companions Gouvernal and Cahedin, Hoel's son.

The master of this picture is the best of the six artists who collaborated on the Romance. Although there is not much to choose between them in quality, he surpasses all the rest in his reproduction of facial expression and the luminosity of his colours, which are harmoniously apposed. His figures are outlined in black and his drapery is modelled partly with dark lines and partly with darker shades of natural colour. He was well versed in contemporary styles of dress. The men wear close-fitting coloured hose and knee-length surcoats gathered at the waist with gold-trimmed belts. The flowing sleeves are typical of Paris fashions during the second decade of the fifteenth century. Collars are high and of a different colour from the coats beneath. The king's forked beard also accords with contemporary fashion. The costumes are bright in colour, and their diversity injects variety into the scene. Only Tristan and his friend in the background wear clothes of the same hue. Iseult's lone female figure forms a harmonious link between the two halves of the composition. Her costume is no less elegant and fashionable than those of her male companions. It falls to the ground in soft folds, and the sleeves, apart from being even fuller than the men's, are lined with some white material – possibly fur. The upper part of her gown, which is gathered with a belt just below the breasts, culminates in a high collar with a narrow ruff. The small tilted head is lovingly painted, and its delicacy contrasts strongly with Tristan's robust and resolute cast of feature. A golden brooch adorns the front of the small red hat, beneath which two bunches of golden curls can be seen.

Our miniature conveys much of the courtly elegance of the Parisian society which, in company with the Duc de Berry, delighted in the artistic embellishment of religious and secular manuscripts. It was also a society which had time to read or listen to readings from lengthy works of this sort, whose illustrations portrayed the ladies and gentlemen of the court either in ceremonial costume or attired for war and the tournament.

This large volume was acquired in France for Prince Eugene of Savoy, who brought it into line with the rest of his library by ordering a red morocco binding for it in Vienna. Still bound in this material, it passed into the Imperial Court Library in 1738.

Plate 45

SENECA

'Tragedies'

369 leaves, $11\frac{1}{4} \times 8\frac{1}{8}$ ins
60 miniatures of various sizes
Flemish master resident in France, *c*. 1420
Cod. 122

DEATH OF ASTYANAX. SCENE FROM THE TRAGEDY 'TROADES' BY SENECA
FOL. 206ᵛ. ORIGINAL SIZE

The silhouettes of the human figures are clearly defined, and drapery is modelled in darker shades of natural colour. One characteristic feature of the landscape is that the hills appear to be constructed of scalloped layers. The foliage of the star-shaped trees is lit with gold, and their trunks glow with reflected golden radiance. There is a noticeable lack of proper perspective in the landscape: the yellow tufts of grass are almost the same height as the trees, and the latter are far too small in relation to the figures.

As in other paintings of this period, legendary figures of the ancient world are portrayed in contemporary French costume, which included the long knee-length coat with belt, high collar and puff-sleeves worn by the messenger on the left of the chorus. The man in the front rank is wearing a surcoat resembling a dalmatic over his red tunic. The hats – circular turban-like affairs, mostly with a pendant scarf attached – are of a type which was to remain in fashion at the Burgundian court until after the middle of the century.

The colours are juxtaposed with great variety and skill, pale shades being preferred.

Details of style enable one to gauge that the miniatures in this book originated under the influence of Parisian court art – during the 1420s to judge by sartorial fashions. Other features point to the Netherlands, notably the windmills which occur in some of the landscapes and the manifest attempt to invest human figures with dramatic animation. All in all, the work is a typical Franco-Flemish product of the first quarter of the fifteenth century.

The book's unpretentious original binding has survived, and with it an autographic entry made by its first owner, who may also have commissioned it. Inscribed on the inside of the front cover are the words: 'Iste tragedie sunt domini Karoli de Francia ducis Biturie. Karolus.' (These tragedies belong to Lord Charles of France, Duke of Bourges. Charles.) Charles, Lord of France and Duke of Bourges, became Charles VII of France (Joan of Arc's king) in 1422, so the book must have been his property before he assumed the throne.

The inside of the back cover bears the date 1570 and the name of Johannes Sambucus, the imperial historiographer, who purchased the book in Paris for twenty-two ducats. It passed into the Imperial Court Library together with his other books, either in 1578 or 1587.

Plate 46

BOOK OF HOURS FRAGMENT

46 leaves, 7⅝ × 5½ ins
3 miniatures with ornamental frames, ornamental borders on every page
numerous initials of various sizes
Paris, *c.* 1420
Cod. 2656

MADONNA IN A ROSE ARBOUR
FOL. 12ʳ. ORIGINAL SIZE

came to Paris from the north. Working in the French capital, he not only produced a substantial number of works with the aid of assistants but acted as instructor to other book illuminators. Stylistically, the present fragment belongs to his early period, i.e., 1420 or shortly thereafter. Among other features typical of this period and a hangover from the fourteenth century is the bright chequered background of blue and gold cubes, which was very popular with Parisian book-painters of the early fifteenth century.

We cannot say with any certainty for whom this book was intended. One of its three miniatures depicts a noblewoman kneeling before the Virgin – undoubtedly the person who commissioned it, though positive identification is impossible. Her purple gown and the brooch of precious stones in her head-dress conform to the fashions of *c.*1420 and indicate that she belonged to the highest social stratum, so she may have been a French or English princess.

The script, of which a few lines can be seen on the page bearing the miniature, is a very uniform French Gothic book minuscule which exactly matches the script used in other books illuminated by the 'Bedford Master'. The scribe was the Parisian calligrapher Johannes Parvi.

It is impossible to ascertain how the book came into the Imperial Court Library, but its presence in the Gentilotti Catalogue implies that it must have been acquired prior to 1723. Its high quality earned it a place among the rare books which Napoleon brought back to Paris, where it received the stamp of the 'Bibliothèque Impériale' in 1809, but it was restored to the Imperial Library in Vienna after 1815.

Plate 47

BOOK OF HOURS

201 leaves, 8⅝ × 6⅛ ins
15 miniatures, very many initials of various sizes, ornamental borders on every page
Paris, *c.* 1420
Cod. Ser. N. 2614

Adoration of the Kings
Fol. 73ᵛ. Original size

The miniature in the present prayer-book depicts the Three Kings as representatives of the three ages of man: old age, manhood, and youth. The picture itself, which has a domed extension at the head, is enclosed by a thin gold frame with an equally thin coloured frame inside it. The scene is set partly in the open, on a stretch of greensward overhung by a dilapidated roof supported on thin posts. In the background stands a hill with a solitary tree sprouting from it, and visible above the roof is a stretch of blue sky and the golden star of Bethlehem.

The Virgin is seated on an upholstered couch with her head resting against a white cushion, wearing a long blue robe and a mantle of the same colour. Her long fair hair cascades loosely over her shoulders and her finely modelled features are tilted in the direction of the Child, who is kneeling in her lap with both arms extended towards the old king. The latter has gone down on his knees and is proffering a gold vessel. He is attired in a gold-embroidered robe with a blue wallet hanging from the belt, but has doffed his crown and laid it on the ground beside him. The other two kings are still standing erect with their crowns on their heads. Their costumes are totally different but of equal splendour. The king in the long red robe and the red and gold coat of mail wears a turban under his crown and a gold wallet at his belt. The youthful king on the right wears a short but sumptuous fur-trimmed doublet and a gold chain adorned with large gold pendants round his neck. His hose and buskins are alternately white and orange – probably a Parisian fashion gimmick of *c*. 1420. Standing unobtrusively in the background with his hands folded is Joseph, a Father-Christmas-like figure with a red hood and white beard.

The picture undoubtedly originated in the atelier of the 'Master of the Duke of Bedford', whose style is particularly evident in the vigorous facial modelling and gorgeous costumes. However, Joseph's face and Mary's somewhat perfunctorily modelled features indicate that this miniature was not the work of the master himself, who invariably depicted Joseph with a forked beard. It thus bears witness to the fact that the 'assistants' of the great Parisian masters were first-rate artists in their own right.

The book came into the National Library in 1936, via the Ambras Collection.

Plate 48

PETRARCH

'On remedies for either kind of fortune'

259 leaves, 14⅛ × 10¼ ins
2 large miniatures, 5 ornamental frames, several ornamental borders and initials
Paris, *c.* 1470
Cod. 2559

MADAME FORTUNE AT HER WHEEL
FOL. 5ᵛ. REDUCED

The French court thought so highly of this artist that all the leading bibliophiles placed their commissions with him. What with his minute attention to detail, elegant colouring and lucid treatment, even of allegorical scenes, he was well able to satisfy the most exacting patron. Most of his settings are symmetrically constructed, and steeply rising floors create an illusion of perspective. The room in the Wheel of Fortune picture is bounded in the background by two windows with coloured circular designs let into the centre of their panes. Surmounting the whole scene is a gilded frame of carved wood supported on either side by pillars.

The narrow gold three-sided frame with its coloured flowers, the initial at the beginning of the text and the broader frame of flowers, foliage, birds and butterflies should probably be attributed to an assistant, while the escutcheon in the lower margin is a later addition. A partly erased note at the end of the work testifies that the original owner was Jacques d'Armagnac, a political agitator who was executed at Paris in 1477. The book was subsequently acquired by Tanneguy du Chatel, Councillor and Chamberlain to Louis XI.

Like many other masterpieces of French book illumination, this manuscript later passed into the collection of Prince Eugene of Savoy, who had it bound in red morocco and blocked in gold, front and back, with a large version of his coat of arms. Red morocco bindings were common to all the historical and literary works in Prince Eugene's library. Scientific treatises were re-bound in yellow morocco and theological works in blue. Many precious old bindings were destroyed in the process, undoubtedly, but the unalloyed elegance of the uniform volumes compensated for this loss. The Imperial Court Library was greatly enriched when, in 1738, the emperor acquired the entire collection from Eugene's heir, the Duchess of Sachsen-Hildburghausen.

Plate 49

BOCCACCIO

'Theseid', French translation

198 leaves, 10½ × 7⅛ ins
16 miniatures, one historiated initial, ornamental borders, many initials
France, *c.* 1455–60
Cod. 2617

THE RELEASE OF ARCITAS
FOL. 64ʳ. ORIGINAL SIZE

preoccupied with the task of releasing him. One of them is kneeling on the ground in an extremely complicated position (note the left sleeve ruckled by the knee) while the man in the bright blue doublet instructs him on how to remove the fetters. The latter is leaning so far forward that his hat obscures his face, but the features of his companion in the green doublet are rendered with great clarity. Of the figures beyond, all that can be seen is half a face and the suggestion of a hat. Also partially visible through the gateway is the lower storey of the keep.

On the left are Arcitas' friends, waiting to escort him home. The grey charger with the blue trappings and black saddle is obviously meant for him. Several of the horsemen have dismounted in order to greet the released prisoner. Their black top-boots have long piked toes and are fitted with rowelled spurs, and their costumes are colourful. The sleeves of the two men standing in the foreground are parti-coloured, red and white in one instance and black and white in the other. All wear woollen hats of the same type, but the leader's is furnished with a magnificent gold tassel. Some of the party have remained in the saddle. The young man on the black horse in the background wears a particularly elegant parti-coloured doublet and a pointed red cap. Several of the group in front of Arcitas, both mounted and dismounted, seem to be looking up at the window from which, invisible to the beholder, Emilia gazes down at her departing admirer.

The painter showed mastery, not only in his use of colour and the richness and lucidity of his composition, but also in his rendering of human physiognomy. The impression of gaiety created by the picture's vivid colouring is tinged with melancholy by the manifest sorrow on the protagonist's face. The faces of the others, whether wholly or partly visible, exhibit careful modelling, and their healthy colouring is in sharp contrast to the prison pallor of Arcitas.

The painter's expert grasp of technique and of the spirit of his composition presupposes a familiarity with the finest works produced prior to about 1450, including those of the Dutch masters and the brothers Van Eyck in particular.

Various attempts have been made to identify the 'Master of René of Anjou' with a named French painter, but in vain. He was already working for King René by the 1430s, and subsequently collaborated on a number of other works written either for or by René himself. He attained his greatest heights in René's own *Livre du Coeur d'amour épris*. The Boccacio probably came into being somewhat earlier. We know of no single work by this master which was not painted for René. This circumstance, coupled with ancient tradition, has given rise to a theory that the pictures were painted by René himself. The notion that a king could have worked as an illuminator – and an illuminator of surpassing talent – seems implausible on the face of it, yet René's personality and career were such that the possibility cannot entirely be discounted.

René was born in 1409, the son of Duke Louis II of Anjou, titular King of Sicily and Count of Provence. His mother, Yolande of Aragon, brought him up partly in Anjou and partly in Provence. In 1419 he married Isabella, heiress to the Duchy of Lorraine, and spent the ensuing years in Nancy. In 1431, having espoused the cause of his brother-in-law, Charles VII of France, in the armed conflicts of the period, he was taken prisoner by the Duke of Burgundy and incarcerated for several years in the tower of Dijon. René was not released until 1437, and seems to have devoted his time in captivity to a profound study of spiritual matters. Several miniatures in a prayer-book of this period bear an affinity to the style of Jan van Eyck and should be regarded as the earliest-known works of the 'René Master'. René paid a number of visits to Northern Italy and Naples in later years. He never managed to assert his claim to the thrones of Naples and Italy, which were linked with the throne of Jerusalem, but he did become familiar with Italian works of art. From the 1450s onwards he divided his time between Anjou and Provence, where he could devote himself to aesthetic pursuits. He commanded performances of mystery plays at Angers, Aix and Tarascon, and took a personal interest in their presentation. He corresponded with poets and scholars and wrote poetry himself, as did officers of his court. He also wrote a treatise on tournaments. His *Mortifiement de vaine plaisance*, completed *c.* 1455, was followed in 1457 by the romance entitled *Livre du Cueur d'amour épris*. The illuminated manuscript of this work came into being some years later. Thus, if the manuscript translation of Boccaccio and its miniatures originated prior to the romance, their date of origin cannot be much earlier than 1455. René died at Aix in 1480.

If René really was the illuminator of this work, he must have collaborated with someone else. The Boccaccio represented a first step towards the illustrations for his own romance, miniatures, which, as in the Boccaccio, far surpassed the text in artistic merit. But, whether René himself was the artist or whether an as yet anonymous 'René Master' did exist, the paintings in question are still among the unexcelled masterpieces of French book illumination.

In 1524 the Boccaccio was in the possession of Archduchess Margaret of Austria, Regent of the Netherlands and daughter of Emperor Maximilian I. It was later transferred to the Imperial Treasury in Vienna, and from there, in 1753, to the Imperial Court Library.

VIII
ILLUMINATION IN THE NETHERLANDS
FIFTEENTH-SIXTEENTH CENTURIES

Plate 50

BIBLE HISTORIALE

2 volumes, 15½ × 11⅝ ins
Volume I: 345 leaves, 2 full-page miniatures, 141 miniatures within text
26 large and many small initials, several marginal borders
Volume II: 262 leaves, 110 miniatures within text
31 historiated initials, 28 large ornamental initials
many smaller initials, several marginal borders
Utrecht, *c.* 1465
Cod. 2771–2

DEATH AND BURIAL OF MOSES (FROM VOLUME I)
FOL. 129ᵛ. ORIGINAL SIZE

right hand indicates the land which Moses can see but is destined never to tread. Moses, whose eyes are fixed on God, is also depicted as an old man with white hair and a white beard. His undergarment is blue, his loose cloak red, and his shoes black. On his head can be seen the golden 'horns' which were his conventional attribute during the Middle Ages and for part of the Baroque period. The scene is based on the Bible's account of Moses' return from Mount Sinai, where he had seen God (Exodus xxxiv, 29): 'And it came to pass, when Moses came down from mount Sinai... that Moses wist not that the skin of his face shone while he talked with him...' The Latin translation, rendered the Hebrew word for 'shine' in another sense, namely, 'to be horned'. Thus the Vulgate, or accepted Latin version, read as follows: 'Moyses... ignorabat quod cornuta esset facies sua ex consortio sermonis dei...' (Moses... did not know that his face was horned from his conversation with God...) The graphic arts often represented these 'horns' as shafts of light, but sometimes adhered to the literal meaning.

Visible beyond the mountain with its overhanging rock face are an expanse of low-lying ground, two castles, and a winding river. The pale sky immediately above the hills on the horizon becomes tinged with a pale blue which gradually gains in intensity.

The second scene is laid beneath the mountain's brown rocky overhang. Moses lies, hands folded, in the open coffin in the foreground. The picture conflicts with the Bible's assertion that none of the Jews knew where Moses was buried, but the artist has included the coffin because it lends colour to the Biblical account of their lamentations. Beyond the sarcophagus stands a dense throng of men and women of various ages, some of them wearing brightly coloured headgear of fanciful design, others merely kerchiefs. The demeanour of the foremost figures clearly conveys their profound sorrow at the law-giver's passing. The man at Moses' head is probably his brother Aaron. Two more figures are seated in the foreground, one depicted from the rear and the other, a woman, with her right hand raised to her tearful eyes. The figures with draped heads and faces are reminiscent of the 'pleurants' on French tombs. White tents of various shapes can be seen beyond the group of mourners.

The entire picture is distinguished by its fresh colouring. All the colours are boldly stressed and stand out luminously against the solid green of ground and background. Faces and drapery are brush-modelled, but a few of the tent outlines seem to have been executed in pencil. The interior modelling of the figures' clothing, much of it extremely elaborate, was also carried out with the brush. There is a striking difference between the healthy glow in the cheeks of the living Moses and the face of his corpse, which is as pale as his folded hands.

Where perspective is concerned, the artist shows far more skill in depicting a landscape which recedes into the distance than in arranging his figures in order of size. The spatial relationship between the pair of figures on the mountain-top and the group in the foreground is not fully defined, but the two scenes are clearly separated by the sloping brown rock face, and the painter has handled them with great vigour and colouristic skill.

This valuable work formed part of the library of Prince Eugene of Savoy, who had both volumes re-bound in blue morocco. It passed to the Imperial Court Library in 1738.

Plate 51

PRIVILEGES OF GHENT AND FLANDERS

390 leaves, 12¾ × 9¼ ins
2 full-page miniatures, 10 large and 3 smaller miniatures
19 ornamental frames, ornamental borders on many pages
65 initials of various sizes, 22 of them with escutcheons
Ghent, after 1453
Cod. 2583

COUNT THOMAS OF FLANDERS AND HIS WIFE JOANNA BESTOWING PRIVILEGES
FOL. 13ʳ. ORIGINAL SIZE

This large volume lists the privileges which the city of Ghent and the County of Flanders received from their overlords in the course of two centuries. It is a remarkable monument to what was, for Ghent, a highly unpleasant episode in its history. In 1453 the citizens of Ghent rebelled against Burgundian sovereignty but were utterly defeated in a battle fought before the walls of their city. Barefoot and clad only in shirts, representatives of the vanquished population were obliged to kneel before their victor, Philip the Good, and sue for peace.

A register of the privileges which had been amassed over the years was compiled in a sumptuously illuminated manuscript book and presented to Philip the Good, intended both as a propitiatory offering and as testimony to the well-established rights of the burghers of Ghent. Since it took some time to produce such a large and lavishly decorated manuscript, and since the last deed of entitlement recorded in it dates from the year 1454, its putative date of origin must be *c.* 1454–55.

Almost all the miniatures depict the bestowal of privileges, but it was left to the artist's imagination to instil variety into their common theme. The very first miniature in the book exemplifies the composition of such scenes and the artist's individual style.

The picture, surmounted by a shallow arched extension, fills the upper part of the page area. Seated on a wide double throne in a spacious throne-room are Count Thomas and his consort Joanna (identified by the accompanying text). Count Thomas II of Savoy married Joanna, daughter and heiress of Count Baudoin VI of Flanders, in 1237, and the privilege referred to was bestowed in 1241. The figures portrayed here are not of the thirteenth century, however, but fifteenth-century contemporaries of the artist attired in the court dress of his period. The count wears a flowing pale red gown brocaded with gold thread and gathered at the waist with a narrow belt, the skirts being slightly parted to reveal a fur lining. Fur trimming is also visible at the count's throat, and above it the tight gold collar of an undergarment. The loose end of his blue head-dress hangs over one shoulder. His right hand rests on his thigh and his left holds the right hand of his consort, whose gaze, like his, is fixed on the kneeling figures below. The train of Joanna's sumptuous blue gown is spread out on the ground in front of her. The hem is trimmed with gold embroidery and ermine, the gown itself low-cut and gathered just below the breasts by means of a gold belt. Visible between the white revers is a red undergarment and a small gold cross suspended from a red two-string necklace. Joanna's hair has been combed back from her forehead and is entirely hidden beneath her tall butterfly-wing head-dress. The throne is upholstered in green material patterned with gold, and the floor-tiles are also green, interspersed with heraldic lilies on a blue ground. The walls of the chamber are of brown brick, the throne is of wood. The perspective and architectural design of the multi-arched structure above the throne are somewhat puzzling. In this manuscript, perspective still conforms to ancient practice. The size of the figures in the room is governed not by their relative position but by their personal importance. Thus the count and countess are depicted on a grand scale while the petitioners and recipients of privileges, though kneeling in the extreme foreground, are pygmies by comparison. The stature of the ladies and gentlemen of the court falls mid-way between these two extremes.

The petitioners are no less carefully attired than the ladies and gentlemen of the court. They are all gazing up at the noble pair except for the blue-robed young man with the green hat draped over his shoulder, who seems to be more interested in the foremost lady-in-waiting, whose long train is draped in the same way as that of the countess. Standing on the left of the throne is the chancellor, with his left hand resting on the pommel of the arm-rest and his right hand holding the privilege, from which dangles a large red seal. Other courtiers stand between him and the doorway, through which blue sky and golden stars can be glimpsed. It was one of the idiosyncrasies of the 'Master of the Privileges of Ghent' that he invariably inserted stars whenever blue sky was visible, and he occasionally went so far as to insert the sun and moon as well.

The courtiers on the left display divers forms of male head-gear, whereas the ladies-in-waiting on the right are wearing several variants of the same tall French-Burgundian head-dress.

For a picture painted *c.* 1454, this miniature is decidedly archaistic in composition. By the end of the 1440s, Philip the Good was already employing the services of artists like the 'Girard Master', who painted pictures in which the laws of perspective were observed to the letter and individual details of human physiognomy conveyed with great cogency. In this book, the retention of an old-fashioned style long abandoned by other painters at the ducal court of Burgundy is countervailed by extremely lavish ornamentation and an abundant use of gold. The delicate draughtmanship of the figures and ornamental borders stamps them as the work of an artist of great ability, even if he did cultivate a style quite unlike that of the masters who were modern in the 1450s. He was probably a pupil of the 'Master of Guillebert de Metz'.

Although the main scenes throughout this work are principally devoted to figures from the past attired in contemporary dress, the marginal ornamentation pays homage to Philip the Good (1419–67) and, in particular, to the Order of the Golden Fleece. Philip founded this order of chivalry in 1429, on the occasion of his marriage to Isabella of Portugal in Bruges. The Golden Fleece was intended to symbolize the lofty, idealized goal which ought to hover before the eyes of every gallant knight. There was, for instance, the Golden Fleece which Jason won in Colchis after many trials; there was the fleece which God, in answer to Gideon's request for a pledge of victory, miraculously steeped in moisture as it lay on dry ground and then kept dry as it lay amid the dew; and, finally, there were sundry other fleeces which the court poets soon discovered in the Bible and in mythological accounts, and interpreted in a way which lent allegorical prestige to the order.

The badge of the order was a small ram's fleece in gold, suspended on a chain. The links of the chain consisted of furisons (fire-steels) with their ends bent inwards to form a 'B' for Burgundy, and flints. The furison had been an emblem of the dukes of Burgundy even before the time of Philip the Good.

The lower margin of the page reproduced here contains Philip's large escutcheon and the chain of the Golden Fleece. Flanking these are two more furisons striking golden sparks from the flints beneath them. Flanking these, in turn, are two inclined escutcheons bearing the arms of Ghent. Lettered in gold above Philip's coat of arms are the words AULTRE NARAY (I will have none other), his motto ever since his marriage to Isabella. The continuation of this motto can be seen on the two vertical scrolls in the right-hand margin, which read: 'tant que je vive' (as long as I live). Above the wattle fence which encloses them are the gold initials 'p' and 'y' (philippe and ysabeau). Taken together, they signify that Philip, who had led a very free and easy life before his marriage, had submitted to the close constraints of married life and intended to remain faithful to his spouse for the rest of his days.

The lion in the right-hand margin supports an escutcheon bearing the arms of Savoy, which belonged to Count Thomas. Above it is another furison complete with flint and sparks.

This manuscript was in Charles V's library at Brussels in 1536. It must have come to Vienna in the course of the seventeenth or eighteenth century, and remained in the treasury of the Hofburg until transferred to the Court Library in 1783.

Plate 52

ROMANCE OF GIRART DE ROUSSILLON

192 leaves, 15¾ × 11¾ ins
53 large miniatures, 153 small miniatures in ornamental frames
Flanders, 1448
Cod. 2549

GIRART DE ROUSSILLON AND HIS WIFE OUTSIDE THE BEDCHAMBER OF THE KING OF FRANCE
FOL. 80ʳ. DETAIL, ORIGINAL SIZE

The name of the artist responsible for the excellent miniatures in the Romance of Girart is unknown. There is documentary evidence that Master Jehan de Wauquelin and his assistant Jacquemin were paid for writing this manuscript and two others at Mons in the year 1448, but all we know about the illuminator is that he was identical with the artist who illuminated the first volume of the Chronicle of Hennegau (Bibl. Royale, Brussels, MS. 9242) and the Romance of Alexander (Bibl. Nationale, Paris, MS. 9342). He undoubtedly had assistants, and it was either he or they who later collaborated on the Chronicle of Jerusalem (Austrian National Library, Cod. 2533).

Jehan de Wauquelin, who ran a thriving scriptorium at Mons, employed a whole series of illuminators whose handiwork can be identified in the numerous manuscripts produced there. The 'Girart Master' was the most able of them all, which was no doubt why Wauquelin entrusted him with the illumination of a manuscript intended as a personal tribute to the ruler who was identified with the hero of this romance.

The author of the French text was Wauquelin himself, who based his version on a Latin original, supplementing it with a list of Girart's miracles and a ballad about Philip of Burgundy. It was typical of the Burgundian court's love of charade that Wauquelin referred repeatedly to the name of the patron to whom he dedicated his translation but never mentioned his own. Nevertheless, he ensured that no disadvantages would accrue to him from his modest 'anonymity' by informing the reader at the end of the main text that anyone who wished to ascertain the Christian name and surname of the author need only string together the initial letters of the first fifteen chapters of the book, to wit, JEHAN VVAUQUELIN.

On its own submission, the text was completed in 1447. Work on the miniatures must have started soon afterwards and was probably completed in 1448, because the record of payment indicates that the book was delivered in that year. It is the finest of the manuscripts mentioned above, qualitatively speaking, because most of its miniatures were painted by the 'Girart Master' himself, whereas most of the other books were illuminated by his assistants.

The Romance of Girart de Roussillon was transferred from the Imperial Treasury to the Court Library in 1783. It was probably among the few items from Maximilian I's Burgundian estate which some member of his dynasty sent or brought back to Vienna long after his death. Indeed, it may have gone there as part of the collection owned by Archduke Leopold Wilhelm, a former Regent of the Netherlands, who appointed Emperor Leopold I his heir in 1662.

Plate 53

BOOK OF HOURS

176 leaves, 7 × 4⅞ ins
13 full-page and 13 half-page miniatures, 25 smaller miniatures
numerous pages with ornamental frames, all other pages with ornamental borders
Flanders, early sixteenth century
Cod. 1887

THE FALL
FOL. 21ʳ. ORIGINAL SIZE

ular 'Fall' displays a certain amount of expertise in this respect, notably in his knowledge and portrayal of the relative proportions of male and female anatomy. Adam has broad shoulders and slender hips. Eve is narrow-shouldered, and the only reminder of earlier medieval essays in nudity is the forward thrust of her stomach and thighs. The faces, too, have been deliberately differentiated. Adam, with his dark, somewhat unkempt hair and short beard, has sharper features than his rosy-checked companion, whose long fair hair hangs to her hips.

Beneath this small picture are the opening words of the 'Hore gloriose uirginis marie…' (Hours of the glorious Virgin Mary). The superscription is lettered in red, the beginning of the text in black. An initial 'D'(omine), composed of branch-work, stands on a large gold panel with a smaller initial 'D'(eus) on a smaller gold panel beneath it.

The ornamental frame consists of a red field enclosed by thin gold lines. On it, constructed of branch-work, are the angel's words of salutation to Mary: AVE GRATIA PLENA DOMINVS TECUM BENEDICTA TV IN MVL(IERIBVS). The centred word-dividers resemble golden nail-heads, and were meant to suggest that the components of the frame had been affixed to a base.

All the full-page miniatures in this prayer-book are located opposite smaller pictures representing their Old Testament 'types'. This original form of iconography is, just what distinguishes it from count-less other books produced in Flanders – mainly at Ghent and Bruges – at about the same period, that is to say, during the first two decades of the sixteenth century. It was jointly embellished by several different artists, all of them anonymous. They were the same artists who produced some of the other great masterpieces of late Flemish book illumination, e.g., the *Hortulus animae*. The artist who painted this little picture of the Fall (and several more miniatures in the same book) is known as the 'Prayer-book Master of *c.* 1500'. Although a number of other works are attributed to him, none of his patrons has been identified. This suggests that he was one of those painters who operated in a small commercial atelier, producing works whose pleasing appearance and popular appeal assured them of a ready market. It is a tribute to the artistic standards of these unknown artists that their work, though unsustained by the prestige of a famous name, still speaks for itself today.

The book was furnished with a sumptuous silver-mounted binding in the sixteenth century. It later passed into Baron von Hohendorf's collection, which was acquired by the Imperial Court Library in 1720.

Plate 54

HOURS OF JAMES IV OF SCOTLAND

245 leaves, 7⅞ × 5½ ins
24 Calendar pages adorned with figurative borders and zodiacal signs in landscapes
18 full-page miniatures, 46 smaller miniatures
numerous ornamental borders in a diversity of styles, many initials of various sizes
Flanders, *c.* 1503
Cod. 1897

KING JAMES IV OF SCOTLAND AT PRAYER
FOL. 24ᵛ. ORIGINAL SIZE

by a stone screen topped with gilded railings. Two men, their faces half obscured by the railings, are peering through them at the king.

The altar-piece takes the form of a triptych in a gilded frame. The central picture is of Christ making the sign of the Cross in blessing – a type very frequently found in Netherlandish book- and panel-paintings. The right-hand wing of the triptych is not visible and the left-hand wing depicts St Andrew.

In the middle of the altar-table, flanked by candlesticks holding burning candles, stands a Gothic reliquary. The altar frontal displays the arms of Scotland supported on a blue ground by two white unicorns. The king's motto – 'In my defens' – is disposed on either side of the helmet, and the escutcheon is encircled by the chain of the Order of the Thistle with its St Andrew pendant. This Scottish order of chivalry, originally instituted in 1087, was headed by the king himself. Its membership was limited to sixteen men, all senior members of the Scottish nobility.

This book was formerly in the possession of Emperor Leopold I (d. 1705). Michael Denis, the imperial librarian, reported in 1790 that Leopold had used it as a child and inscribed his name in it. The book was re-bound shortly afterwards, so Leopold's inscription has not survived.

Plate 55

CROY HOURS

181 leaves, 7⅝ × 5⅜ ins
24 Calendar pages with miniatures, 15 full-page miniatures
with ornamental frames in various styles, 19 small paintings of saints
blank margins on all unframed pages adorned with flowers, butterflies, and mythical creatures
Flanders, *c.* 1510
Cod. 1858

JOSEPH AND MARY SEEKING SHELTER AT THE INN
FOL. 55ᵛ. ORIGINAL SIZE

'Eu voz bonnes prieres se recommande celuy qui votre bonne grace demande. De Lalaing.'
(He who solicits your favour commends himself to your devout prayers. De Lalaing.)

Entries were also made by two members of the Croy family who enjoyed the personal friendship of Maximilian and his daughter. Charles de Croy (d. 1527) was godfather to Prince Charles, later Emperor Charles V. His entry read as follows:

'Affin che je soye de vous recommande aceste bonne dame cest
mis sy en enscript votre bon mestre Charles'
(That I be commended by you to this noble lady,
your good Master Charles has here set himself down in writing)

Guillaume de Croy (d. 152x) inscribed the following lines:

'Tant quen ce mondt viveray
parent et amy vous seray CROY'
(For as long as he shall live in this world,
CROY will remain your cousin and friend)

These two 'Croy' entries later gave their name to the whole book, although Archduchess Margaret may be assumed to have been its owner.

The binding of the Croy Prayer-book matches its outstanding pictorial decoration. Its brown leather cover is adorned with gilded silver fittings and blocked in large with the name of its binder, Ludovicus Bloc.

The first record of the book's presence in the Imperial Court Library dates from the beginning of the eighteenth century.

Plate 56

ROTHSCHILD HOURS

252 leaves, 9 × 6¼ ins
12 Calendar pages with miniatures, 67 full-page miniatures, 5 small miniatures
141 pages with ornamental frames, numerous initials of various sizes
Flanders, *c.* 1510–20
Cod. Ser. N. 2844

St Bernard kneeling before the Virgin
Fol. 245ᵛ. Original size

'Bernard, accept my son, the redeemer of all the world!' At the same time, she sprinkled Bernard with a few drops of milk squeezed from her breast, just as though he were the blood-brother of the divine Child.

This episode is a poetic illustration of the heartfelt devotion to the Virgin which St Bernard manifested in his life and writings. To artists, it was a rewarding theme which continued to be used until well into the Baroque period.

Plates 57 and 58

HOURS OF MARY OF BURGUNDY

187 leaves, 8⅞ × 6⅝ ins
24 Calendar pictures, 20 full-page miniatures, 14 historiated initials
16 small paintings of saints, 78 pages with ornamental frames
all other pages with marginal borders,
lower margins of pages without ornamental frames
adorned with painted or pen-drawn drolleries
Bruges, *c.* 1467–80

ADORATION OF THE VIRGIN IN A GOTHIC CHURCH INTERIOR
FOL. 14ᵛ. ORIGINAL SIZE

CRUCIFIXION OF CHRIST
FOL. 43ᵛ. ORIGINAL SIZE

such as this was decorative, and its artistic merit earned it a well-deserved place in the same category as panel-paintings by great artists. We may rest assured, therefore, that the book seldom had an opportunity to distract the thoughts of the devout lady in question.

The two pictures reproduced here, with their 'view-from-a-window' theme, were painted by an artist known as the 'Master of Mary of Burgundy'. The first depicts the lofty choir of a Gothic church as seen through a window. A gold altar-piece, flanked on either side by three gold carrying-poles, stands out against the neutral stone-colour of the architecture. Seated in front of the altar is the Virgin with the Child on her lap. The strong blue of the flowing, richly draped cloak effectively stresses the central figure. Small angels supporting golden candlesticks have alighted on the gold-patterned carpet. A young man wearing a gold cowl and a red cloak lined with yellow kneels on the right, swinging a censer in the direction of the Child. On the left, also kneeling, is a young woman clad in a magnificent fur-trimmed gown of gold brocade and a tall pointed hat draped with a white veil. Her hands are folded in prayer and her right arm clasps a red-bound book to her breast. Behind her are three female attendants, two on their knees and one standing.

The two figures beside the altar in the background are seemingly engaged in conversation, and there is a suggestion of more figures beside the windows of the oratories on either side of the choir.

If the lady kneeling before the Virgin is Mary of Burgundy, the man swinging the censer must be Archduke Maximilian, who married the Burgundian heiress in 1477.

The illusion of watching a scene in church through an open window is further heightened by the masterly perspective of the chamber in the foreground, whose depth is conveyed by the two open casements with their bull's-eye panes. Inside the sill, running the full depth of the church wall, is a window-seat. On this lie a gold chain with pearl pendants and two carnations. The vase of tall irises has been placed on the extreme right so as not to obstruct the view, and the few leaves and petals that overlap the window-frame act as a further aid to perspective.

There is something irresistibly appealing about the figure of the young woman engrossed in her book, and her features are rendered with such individuality that the picture can only be a portrait. The hair is drawn back tightly from the brow and temples and concealed beneath the tall head-dress. The latter is adorned with a pattern in gold and colour, part of which appears to consist of letters – possibly R I A. The white veil falls from the pointed head-dress in soft folds. A similar veil, through which gold necklaces can be seen, covers the lady's broad décolletage. Her golden-brown dress has a deep collar like that of the lady inside the church and is encircled by a broad brocade belt. A grey lap-dog sits comfortably in her lap, and above it, held in both her hands and half propped on the window-seat, is a large book with patterned gilt edges, green binding, and a green cloth wrapper. It lies open at a page commencing with an initial 'O'. A cushion covered with gold brocade reposes on the seat opposite.

The supposition that the lady at the window is also Mary of Burgundy seems plausible but cannot be said with absolute certainty.

The second window picture is no less fascinating. Instead of an interior, it depicts a deep landscape peopled with a variety of figures. The central theme is the crucifixion of Christ, whose feet and right hand have already been nailed to the cross on the ground. Two myrmidons are engaged in nailing his left hand to the cross-beam. Mary (left) is so overcome with grief that she has tried to hurl herself at her son and is being restrained by John. In the immediate foreground, half obscured by the ledge of rock beyond the sill, stands a group of elegantly dressed women, one of them carrying a small child and two with their heads turned to look up at the open window. The two Jewish dignitaries on their right appear to be discussing the proceedings, and in front of them stand two helmeted soldiers. Two female mourners can be seen on the extreme left, and in the middle distance, right and centre, are men on horseback, some richly dressed and all gazing at the scene in the foreground. The soldier with the stick (half left) is keeping some over-eager spectators at bay.

Bordering the patch of sea in the background are the vague silhouettes of buildings and, on the right, an overhanging cliff. Somewhat nearer, the tall crosses destined for the two malefactors jut out into the sky. The crowds around and beyond these two crosses are blurred with distance, and the sky with its light scattering of clouds fades as it nears the horizon. The only substantial area of cloud is situated behind the malefactor's cross on the right.

There is a sharp contrast between the still-life in the window and the tragic drama of the main scene. The cushion on the sill is almost identical with the one on the empty window-seat in the first picture. On it reposes a pearl necklace with various pendants. Lying on the left-hand window-seat is the open jewel-box of the lady who has just left her place beside the window. Hanging out of the casket is a gold chain with a pearl pendant, beside it lies a ring, and leaning against the wall is a small flask with a labelled stopper. The seat opposite is largely obscured by a book opened at a picture of the Crucifixion. The binding and cloth wrapper are black, the markers green.

The pillars on either side of the window appear to be constructed of polished stone, and flanking them on the inner walls of the chamber are stone statues overhung by Gothic baldachins and mounted on pedestals supported by angels. The group on the left represents Abraham being prevented by an angel from killing his son; on the right, Moses points to the brazen serpent on the end of his raised staff. Both these scenes from the Old Testament presage Christ's death on the Cross.

The second window picture exhibits the same merits as the first: painstaking attention to detail, grandiose overall composition, and a masterly command of perspective. What particularly impresses one in the second picture is the artist's handling of the crowd scene. As the figures gradually decrease in density towards the foreground, so the vaguely suggested features of those in the distance gradually yield to faces which are visible in every detail.

This masterpiece must have originated in about 1480, though many of the other pictures – and possibly the text – may have been produced before that. The artists who painted the other miniatures were active at an earlier stage, whereas the 'Master of Mary of Burgundy' did not make his contribution to the work until Charles the Bold was dead, i.e., after 1477. Maximilian married Mary in the same year, and it is almost certain that the figures portrayed in the first window picture are those of the artist's patrons.

A veil of uncertainty will continue to shroud the identity of the artist and his subjects, but there is no doubt that this work conveys all the charm of Flemish book illumination in a most exemplary manner.

The book came into the Imperial Court Library through the agency of Emperor Matthias I (1612–1619), who had been Regent of the Netherlands until 1580.

IX
LATE ILLUMINATION
SIXTEENTH CENTURY

Plate 59

HOURS OF WILLIAM IV OF BAVARIA

212 leaves, $8\frac{1}{4} \times 5\frac{7}{8}$ ins
Armorial page, Calendar adorned with zodiacal signs and monthly occupations
41 miniatures, most of them full-page, numerous initials of which many historiated
numerous figurative borders and frames
Nuremberg, 1535
Cod. 1880

St Anne with the Holy Family
Fol. 184ᵛ. Original size

defenders of the Catholic faith among the German princes, and it was he who summoned the Jesuits to Ingolstadt in 1542. Consequently, while this prayer-book takes good care to embody all the Catholic prayers and all the saints venerated by the Catholic church, its modes of artistic expression – particularly in regard to costume – are reminiscent of the art of the Reformation.

Although the illuminator of the book was himself an adherent of the Reformation, he fulfilled his patron's wishes by painting miniatures associated with the worship of saints. The scribe's name is unknown. Close scrutiny of the text discloses several passages of a puzzling nature. Many of the prayers addressed to individual saints are prefaced by saintly legends inscribed in red, and whole lines of this red script are nothing more than an arbitrary jumble of letters. The script on these pages is indistinguishable from the script on normal pages, and its meaninglessness only becomes apparent on closer inspection. Corrupt passages of a similar kind occur in the introductions to the indulgential prayers, which record the extent of papal indulgences. One can only surmise that this was the scribe's way of protesting against hagiolatry and the doctrine of indulgences – confident that, since miniatures were the book's chief decorative feature, some time would elapse before his client discovered the garbled lines.

It may be that Duke William subsequently presented the book to a Protestant, because several other passages referring to indulgences, though correctly written by the scribe, were later mutilated by erasure. The next owner was Archduchess Magdalena of Austria, who founded the Noblewomen's Convent at Hall in the Tyrol in 1569. Her name, 'Matelena', is inscribed on the fly-leaf. The book passed into the Imperial Court Library when the College was dissolved during the reign of Joseph II.

Plate 60

BOOK OF HOURS

96 leaves, 7⅛ × 4¾ ins
11 large, many smaller miniatures
135 large and small initials, coloured line-fillings
Northern France, 'School of Fontainebleau', c. 1570
Cod. Ser. N. 13,241

THE WOMAN CLOTHED WITH THE SUN (REVELATIONS XII, 1–5)
FOL. 15ᵛ. ORIGINAL SIZE

'Ora pro nobis et defunctis, Sanctissima dei genetrix' (Pray for us and the dead, most holy Mother of God).

The ornamental frame has a gold ground adorned with carnations, strawberries, violets, and other flowers. The large escutcheon at the foot of the page is a later addition, and was overpainted on another coat of arms which can no longer be identified. The existing escutcheon belonged to Henry III (1574–1589) in his capacity as King of Poland, not of France. Henry III, third son of Henry II of France and Catherine de Médicis, was elected King of Poland in 1572, after the death of Sigismund Augustus, the last of the Jagellons. Having been crowned in Cracow on 15 February 1574, he left Poland on 18 June of the same year to assume the French throne in succession to his brother Charles IX (1560–74). Thus, the new coat of arms must have been added in the period between February and June 1574. The book itself was designed as a royal gift in honour of the Polish coronation. The escutcheon is quartered: the first and fourth quarters bear the Polish eagle and Knight of Lithuania in silver on a red ground, the second and third a trio of gold fleurs-de-lys on a blue ground. Encircling the escutcheon is the chain of the Order of St Michael, with pendant, and surmounting it the crown of Poland, its hoop adorned with an apple and a cross.

The rest of the miniatures in this book still adhere to the decorative scheme which had been prescribed for such works since the fourteenth century. One iconographic rarity is the picture for Vespers, which customarily portrayed the Flight into Egypt but is here devoted to the return of the Holy Family *from* Egypt.

Stylistically, these miniatures can only be compared with panel-paintings and frescoes, since no other examples of contemporary book illumination survive. Their style is unmistakably related to the art of the French court during the second half of the sixteenth century, a period when all the artists in court service congregated at Fontainebleau, the contemporary French art centre. They were mostly Italians who had imported Mannerism into France from their native Florence, Bologna or Parma, and had found willing pupils there. The spherical cloud-masses in the picture reproduced here, together with the numerous angelic figures emerging from or half obscured by the sky's multiple gradations of grey and blue, are late descendants of the swirling clouds and angels on the cupola of Parma Cathedral, and the dainty figure and elongated features of the woman clothed with the sun accord with the Mannerist treatment of the female form. The painting's richly varied tonality and successful interplay of light and shade bear witness to the artist's brilliant technique.

Although produced for use in the diocese of Rouen, the book did not necessarily originate there. While its place of origin cannot be specified beyond doubt, however, the artist who painted it almost certainly belonged to the 'School of Fontainebleau'.

The book was re-bound in Vienna at the beginning of the nineteenth century, probably at the time of its presentation to Emperor Francis of Austria, in whose personal library it used to be. It was acquired by the Austrian National Library in 1920.

INDEX